TRUST *and* FOLLOW

TRUST *and* FOLLOW

LEARNING HOW TO BE CEO
OF A GOD-OWNED BUSINESS

JOHN HOUSTON

Forefront
BOOKS

Published by Forefront Books.
Distributed by Simon & Schuster.

Library of Congress Control Number: 2023909493

Print ISBN: 978-1-63763-134-8
E-book ISBN: 978-1-63763-135-5

Cover Design by Bruce Gore, Gore Studio, Inc.
Interior Design by Bill Kersey, KerseyGraphics

*T*o my wife, kids, and team members who have been a part of building the John Houston Family of Companies.

Working alongside you has been one of the greatest blessings in my life.

CONTENTS

INTRODUCTION

"*T*rust Me," God said. "Stop relying on yourself, and trust Me."

He told me to trust Him when my big brother and I were living on our own as teenagers and later when He introduced me to my future wife, Tracy. He told me to trust Him when Tracy and I filed for bankruptcy and when my mother took her life, when I started a homebuilding company and when the housing crash followed two years later.

"Trust Me."

It's one of the hardest things imaginable, to trust an invisible God more than the cash in my wallet or my own hard-won experience. For more than thirty years He's been teaching me to let go of the things I relied on. I'm still learning.

One of the greatest stories in history is the exodus of God's chosen people from Egypt through the desert to the promised land—a two-week journey that took forty years. God used those years to prepare the people by cleansing them of cultural influences they had lived with for four hundred years—most importantly their constant desire to worship and depend on something other than Him. He told them to trust Him, and some of the time they did.

God gave them food every day. Manna, He called it, and He gave them just enough for that day, except for the day before the Sabbath, when He gave them enough food for two days. He was teaching them to rely on Him—not themselves or any barns—for food.

In the New Testament, Jesus told His disciples, "Do not be afraid, . . . for your Father has been pleased to give you the kingdom. Sell your possessions and give to the poor. Provide purses for yourselves that will not wear out, a treasure in heaven that will never fail, where no thief comes near and no moth destroys. For where your treasure is, there your heart will be also" (Luke 12:32–34).

"Do not worry!" He tells us again and again. "Trust Me. Your treasure in heaven will not fail."

Through Jesus, God has offered grace and forgiveness to me as He's prepared me through my own "exodus" journey, stripping away many of the things that stand between me and Him and giving me opportunities to discard others. Little did I know that as these things were removed from my life, God would replace them with things far greater and more valuable, primarily a deeper relationship with Him and with others.

In my prayer time, I felt God asking me to give Him our homebuilding company.

I thought I had already given God everything—the company, my marriage, our children, every relationship in my life. I had prayed to God countless times, saying that everything was His. Whenever I talked to people about John Houston Homes, I made it clear that it was God's company.

This was different. God was asking me to give Him the company. Literally.

Other than Jesus Himself and my wife and children, John Houston Homes was the most important thing in my life—the thing that, with God's help, we had built from nothing into one of the one hundred largest homebuilding companies in the United States.

He had given us our purpose: to reach people for Christ and give to His kingdom. We were building and selling hundreds of homes every year south of Dallas, and we had tried to do it all with God's purpose at the heart of every decision we made.

I had told myself that my identity was not in my company—that I was not defined by what I did but by who I am: a child of God.

Then why was God's request so difficult?

The truth is, I had poured so much into this company for almost twenty years, and now God was asking me to give it to Him.

Through prayers and counsel with my wife, our executive leadership team, and my pastor, I came to understand that God wanted me to no longer be owner of the company and to let our employees become the owners through an employee stock ownership plan. Over time, they would take full authority. In the meantime, I would remain in leadership as CEO.

God wasn't firing me. He wasn't taking anything from me. He was asking me to give myself to Him fully and completely. He was asking me to trust Him fully with the company that I already called His—to completely take my hands off the wheel. To let others step up and lead.

If you're an entrepreneur or high-level leader, you know how hard this is.

As I write this book, I am still in the process of transitioning out of my role as CEO, and God has given me a surprising peace. God has a new thing in mind for me. By the time you're reading this, the process will be complete.

A favorite Bible verse of mine in this season has been 2 Corinthians 3:2–3 (MSG): "Your very lives are a letter that anyone can read by just looking at you. Christ himself wrote it—not with ink, but with God's living Spirit; not chiseled into stone, but carved into human lives—and we publish it."

So this book is God's story that He has carved into our lives—me, Tracy, our children, our executive leaders, our employees, vendors, and subcontractors. This is the story of how God prepared our hearts for greater capacity to trust and follow Him. As I reflect on these stories, I am in awe of God and what He's done. I think, *Man, is this what a full, abundant life looks like?* Then I hear the Lord say, "This is as full and abundant as you are aware of today, but trust Me and keep following Me, and I will continue to reveal My full, abundant life for you."

My hope for you as you read these stories is that you can look back on your own life and see the stories God has been writing with your life as you learn to trust and follow Him.

THE BEGINNING
OF TRUST

*T*wo decades ago, I was the youngest person in the room at my first meeting as a member of our church's board of elders—maybe the youngest ever who had served on the board. The others had been talking for months about a major building project, and that night they planned to approve a $5 million loan for construction. I was seeing the details for the first time, so I explained that I wouldn't be able to vote for it that night.

Our pastor, Rev. Tom Wilson, asked me to trust the other members of the board and vote with them. They had been working on this and praying about it for a year already, and God had given them direction.

It wasn't that I didn't trust them, I said. Of course I did. And I understood that they were just trying to get the deal done after all the work they had done. I also completely trusted Pastor Tom, who had shown my wife, Tracy, and me the love of Christ when we faced our deepest pain.

"But God put me on this board," I said with a tone that probably came across as harsh and maybe even arrogant, "and I'm ultimately accountable to Him, not to you."

That was the way I talked to people. My friends. My coworkers. Tracy. And in this case, my elders and my pastor. I didn't respect them as I should have, and that came out in my words and my tone.

Some of the elders expressed their frustration with me, and so did Pastor Tom. The board certainly could have approved the loan without my vote, but—and this is one of the things I love about our church—our board believes if we aren't unanimous in what we believe God is telling us to do, we don't move forward.

Then Pastor Tom said something like, "John, we understand you don't have experience working with numbers this big."

Well, that ticked me off, and I probably wasn't as gentle as I needed to be. At that time, I had significant responsibilities in my job with the Annuity Board of the Southern Baptist Convention. "Do you understand that I work with an investment company, and we work with $50 million a year?" I asked. "My decision has nothing to do with that. It's about the stewardship, how I am going to steward the responsibilities the Lord has given me. I'm not going to stand before you in heaven. I'm going to stand before the Lord."

And that's pretty much how my first board meeting ended.

Pastor Tom's son, Scott, was his associate and my dear friend, and he quickly stepped in as an intermediary between his dad and me. I had gummed up the whole system, and I hadn't voiced my perspective in a loving way. I also knew that Satan wants to try to bring division to relationships, especially between Christians. In this case he was diverting my attention from what God called me to do, because if he could distract me a little bit and get me frustrated, then he would be winning. It wasn't that what I was saying was incorrect, but the tone, attitude, and approach were wrong.

Before the next meeting, I studied the plans and the loan. I spent time in prayer, and God made it clear that He wanted me to vote my approval for the loan. A few days later, we met again and voted in one accord.

God spent years teaching me to seek and trust the Spirit-led wise counsel of other followers—as long as it lines up with the Word of God—the way Pastor Tom asked me to trust the board that night. I had been so sure of my own understanding. Through that process, the Lord began to build trusting relationships between me and many of the men on the church board. We faced more opportunities together and witnessed the Lord revealing Himself in amazing ways.

STARTING
THE BUSINESS

When God told me to start a homebuilding company to reach people for Christ and give to the kingdom, I had never built a house. But I was filled with the confidence I had displayed at my first church board meeting. In my role at the Annuity Board of the Southern Baptist Convention, I had learned about budgets and project management. Years earlier, a custom homebuilder in my hometown of Waco had hired me to do framing and concrete work, but I still didn't know much about construction.

God made it clear that building houses was to be a vehicle for achieving His purpose, not the purpose itself.

What I didn't know was that He would have me wait for five years before He said, "Now, start!" But in those five years, as we prayed, sought wise counsel, prepared, and waited on Him, He built a firmer spiritual foundation underneath Tracy and me. He continued to prepare my heart and mind in ways that I did not always appreciate or even see at the time.

At the annuity board, I was working with numbers, which I enjoyed, and then I was transferred to legal and compliance, becoming the liaison between the business and information technology, which I hated.

In my new role, however, I was learning skills that I would need to run a company, and I was also learning perseverance. Almost every day, I prayed, *God, help me do this job well and with the right attitude, because I don't want to be doing it.* And He did help me. I learned to walk closer to Him and take joy in my relationship with Him. Years later, that closer relationship built over my five years of waiting would sustain me through the valleys when the housing market collapsed.

THE WORST PLACE TO START BUILDING HOMES

When God told me to start the homebuilding business, and I did my research to put the business plan together, I learned that Dallas–Fort Worth was one of the hardest places in the country to build homes and make money.

And the hardest area of Dallas–Fort Worth to build new homes and make money was south of Dallas, which is where we were. So it made zero sense to start the company there. I talked with builders and with experts in the industry, and they all told me that south of Dallas was the last place in the United States they would start building because the margins were so tight. It was almost impossible to make a profit.

But all we knew was that God was telling me to build houses south of Dallas. This was where we lived and where we had our church home.

Several of the men who had been in my first church board meeting became wise counselors to me as I started the company. They guided me and prayed with me through important milestones as we built our first homes.

With a brand-new company, and a bankruptcy in my past, I had limited access to money from banks. After I asked two other banks for loans, the Lord opened an amazing door with Vintage Bank, which gave me my first construction loan to build my first house. We still work with them. We did not borrow money for business operations—only for construction. We saw that as an investment rather than debt—the loan was backed by the value of the house, and we paid it back after the sale. Then Southwest Securities allowed me to borrow enough money to build more homes. Again, I repaid the loan when we closed the sale. Over time I expected to earn the trust of both banks so we could borrow more money to build more homes.

Then an opportunity arose where some of my friends from the board of elders became more than advisers to me. About eighteen months after I started building houses, I heard about a subdivision in our area being developed by Hillwood, a company founded by Ross Perot Jr. Hillwood was one of the premier development companies in Texas, and they were developing Harmony, a 166-acre master-planned community in Red Oak, right in our backyard. It was one of the first master-planned communities in Ellis County. As you would expect from a Perot company, the quality of the infrastructure and amenities at Hillwood were top-notch. I reached out to them, and when they invited me to buy fifty lots and build on them, I was excited for the opportunity.

I was virtually unknown, and the "halo effect" of building in Harmony could be significant. Developers and customers would rightfully assume that Hillwood had done its homework on me and my company and determined that I was a quality builder. Otherwise, they wouldn't let me into their community. That implied endorsement would go a long way for my young company.

Problem was, I needed money to build more homes. Hillwood wanted $320,000 earnest money on the lots, and they expected me to build several spec homes and a model home. Plus, I would need another $50,000 to scale up my operations to build more homes.

Even with Hillwood's endorsement, I didn't have a relationship with a bank that would allow me to borrow that kind of money, nor did I want to borrow money for operations.

One more thing: I wasn't taking any money out of the company at this point—no salary, no draws, nothing except what we needed to pay our tithe and our offering (gifts to the kingdom over and above our tithe) and taxes. We were living solely on Tracy's salary from working in information technology at JCPenney. At night, Tracy was keeping the financial books for our company, also for no pay. Later I would look back and understand that it wasn't that God didn't want to pay us. Rather, He was increasing my dependence on Him and reminding us that this was His business and for His glory.

In the meantime, I needed $370,000.

I was also in a prayer group with some of the men who served on the elder board, and we had become good friends. I told a couple of those guys about my opportunity with Hillwood and asked if they would be interested in investing money in this Hillwood community or if they knew anybody who would want to. They all knew, of course, that my company was barely older than a start-up. We had built about twenty homes, and they believed in what I was doing. And the Hillwood brand association didn't hurt there either.

But writing a big check and investing in this community wasn't a no-brainer. They went home and prayed, asking God for direction. They talked with their wives and sought their own wise counsel.

Let me also say that these guys were not extremely wealthy. It wasn't like they would be taking a small percentage of their stock portfolio and diversifying into real estate. They were hard-working, faithful, godly people who had saved money along the way, and they followed God's lead. Some of them made the investment, and they recruited others until I had the money I needed. A wife of one of the men was a teacher, and she borrowed money from her retirement account to lend to me. Pastor Tom also offered to invest. They knew there was a risk, of course, but I honestly believe it was God's favor that led them to invest in what He had asked us to do. Otherwise, it didn't make sense for them to write those checks. My financial commitment to them was to use the first 25 percent of profits from the sale of each home to pay back the investment. At that rate, I would be able to get their investment back pretty quickly. I felt a huge responsibility to them.

I drove to the Hillwood office in Dallas to sign the contract, and we went into a conference room with a huge, beautiful table. I sat down, and Fred Balda, president of Hillwood, said, "John, I just want to make sure you understand that the people you're building alongside are some of the toughest competitors in Dallas–Fort Worth. So, before we sign this contract, I want to know that you're clear about that, and you're confident that this is what you want to do."

I already had considered what he was telling me. We would be building some of the smallest homes in Harmony on the smallest lots alongside some huge national builders. I was young and was just trying to follow Jesus. He was opening doors for me, and I trusted Him to walk through them with me. At that moment, as I sat at that table, I felt strongly the Holy Spirit speaking to me, "Don't forget, you don't fight against flesh and blood. You fight against darkness, and I will take care of you as you follow Me."

Then I felt the Lord say, "You're going to build circles around these guys because everywhere you put a house, I will surround that house and protect it."

The Lord was not telling me that my competitors represented darkness. Far from it. He was showing me the darkness in my own heart, the thorn in my own flesh—greed that was rooted in my lack of trust in Him. This would be a years-long struggle, maybe a lifelong struggle, because God is such a merciful, generous Father, He doesn't just reach in and yank out the thorn. It has been a process that continues today as He helps me clean up the residue.

God was giving me encouragement, reminding me that if I focused on Him and His light, the Light of the World, then the darkness would never overcome it.

I signed the documents and walked out of the building thinking, *Oh, no, God, I hope I heard Your voice!* But I was also excited because I believed I truly had heard Him.

SELLING HOMES AND BUILDING COMMUNITY

With fifty lots and high expectations from Hillwood, we couldn't rely on home-by-home financing anymore. I went back to our banker at Southwest Securities and explained that money from our investors had allowed us to make a commitment to Hillwood with $320,000 earnest money. I asked for a line of credit so we wouldn't have to present a new loan application every time we had another home to start. They agreed to a $2 million line, which allowed us to build a model home and a few spec houses. Everywhere I turned, God was helping me build a network of relationships to grow the company faster than I ever could have done alone while also building my faith that He was with me. I was literally seeing that faith without works is dead, but as we seek first the kingdom of God and His righteousness, He will provide all our needs according to His will (Matthew 6:33).

Suzette and Jason Crow were an early example of God providing all our needs. They were at home in Plano watching *Hot On! Homes*, a Dallas TV show that features new homes and communities around the metroplex. The show mentioned John Houston Homes and our entry into Harmony, and Suzette felt a stirring in her spirit that she still cannot explain. She thought God might want them to move into one of our homes.

She told Jason what she was thinking and said, "I don't understand it. It's just what I feel."

"Well, I'm not going to say that you're not hearing from the Lord," Jason said. But Suzette could tell he was skeptical. And why not? She wasn't so sure herself. They had never heard of me or the company.

That afternoon they drove from Plano to Red Oak, about forty miles, and stepped into our model home, where Rob Poole was our salesman.

Suzette was a commercial lender at a bank at the time, selling loans to her customers. As a salesperson herself, she had a heightened sensitivity to people who were "salesy."

Rob was the exact opposite of that. "He asked the right questions and really cared for us," Suzette remarked. "Our experience confirmed for me that this was what the Lord wanted us to do."

She told Jason right there in the model home, "I think this is the neighborhood that we need to live in, and this is the house we need to buy, and we need to work with Rob."

Jason agreed, and they wrote a deposit check for their new home.

Another time a couple stepped into our model home and told Rob that they had just signed a contract to buy a house in the subdivision across the street. Driving away, they saw our homes and felt God was urging them to come and look. Rob shared with them the vision of our company, and they said, "We just bought the wrong house. We're going to cancel the contract. We'll be right back."

Yet another couple was driving down I-35, saw our sign, and felt like the Lord was telling them they needed to go look at that neighborhood. And they weren't even in the market for a new home! They walked in and told Rob, "We don't even know why we're here."

We prayed over each house we were building and fasted many times, asking God, *Please bring the people here that You want us to reach for Christ and help us to sell homes right on time so we can give to the kingdom.*

Many of the homes we built in Harmony were one-story, 1,800-square-foot homes. Other builders were selling homes that were 3,800 to 4,000 square feet. We were comfortable with our market, and we were filling a need for Hillwood.

Even after people moved into their homes, they dropped by the model home to visit with Rob. I was in the Harmony model home looking over some plans one afternoon when Suzette and Jason Crow came in. We hadn't met, and I think they were a little taken aback when I invited them to our house for "Fight Night." Pretty regularly, Tracy and I would invite friends to our house to watch UFC on pay-per-view as an opportunity to reach people for Christ who might not step into a church but would come to watch a UFC fight. We were building relationships with them, and many times they would accept Christ and begin going to church. It usually turned out that the guys would stay in the living room and watch the fight, and the women would sit on the back porch with coffee or tea. We invited friends from church and work and the neighborhood. In fact, everybody got so comfortable with the routine that when I was out of town, they organized the event themselves at our house. Tracy and I loved that. Building community this way gave us opportunities to reach people for Christ.

For our first five years in business, 92 percent of our sales came from customer referrals. When we took care of people, they told their sister or aunt or cousin or friend about us.

Our approach to home warranties was a huge driver of referrals and reflected our overall mindset. New homes generally carried a one-year warranty, and most builders honored the warranty until the expiration date but not one day more. Warranty repairs, to them, represented expenses with no corresponding income stream.

We couldn't operate that way. Our customers were our neighbors and friends. If they had a problem sixteen months after they moved in, we wanted to help them. We quickly learned that when we took care of them, they took care of us. When we addressed issues that came up after the warranty expired, that kind of "second-mile" service really stood out with customers. It might have cost us some money along the way, but the customer referrals were way more effective, dollar for dollar, than any marketing campaign. As for stewardship, I am not saying that we fixed everything a customer asked us to fix, but if it was something warrantable but past the expiration date, then we generally went above and beyond and took care of it. If the customer had something outside of warranty, then we would try to connect them with a good, reputable company we had relationship with to help them get it repaired. It was about serving the customer while still being a good steward with what the Lord entrusted to us.

A MODEL OF LOVE, A LESSON IN WISE GIVING

*B*efore I started the homebuilding company, God brought Justin and Andrea Lathrop to serve as pastors in our church. Tracy and I quickly became friends with them. Soon after I started the company, I began looking for someone to help with part-time office work. Andrea joined us, and she was a perfect fit. Tracy and I became even closer friends with her and Justin, who was having a powerful impact on our church.

Over time Justin also had an impact on me by his words and the way he modeled living by love. He had an amazing way of making connections and building relationships with almost anybody. He even wrote a book, *The Likeable Christian: A Journey Toward the Radical Love Jesus Taught Us to Live*. "As Christians," he wrote, "I think we're called to be likeable."

Then he explained what he meant. "My objective is to get us to think about how we can, as Christians, exude great love—the kind of love Jesus showed to people of all backgrounds, lifestyles, and beliefs—even as we live with strong convictions."

Justin and Andrea were living out that belief long before he wrote his book. God was using them to begin a transformation in my heart before I knew what was happening. Andrea was the first of dozens, maybe hundreds, of relationships God has brought at just the right time into my life and our company.

Our growing small company started creating opportunities for us to give to God's kingdom, and at times our giving was not very wise—we donated without stewarding the giving as diligently as we would when dealing with business financials.

As the business grew, we were able to give beyond our tithe to the church and other nonprofits. Through a US ministry, we began financially supporting a Christian orphanage in Africa. Tracy visited the orphanage and brought home stories of the impact they were having on the children. We were good friends with the American leaders of the ministry and were excited to work with them.

I didn't have a chief financial officer at the time, and one morning my accountant called and said he didn't have a contribution statement from the ministry.

I called my friend at the ministry, and he said he would get it, but he didn't. After several more calls, he finally admitted, "We don't know how much you gave us."

"What are you talking about?" I said.

"We're not that great at keeping records," he said. "Check your records and tell us how much you gave, and we'll write a receipt."

Of course, we had canceled checks, but that wasn't the point.

I knew then that I needed somebody to help us be wiser and better stewards in our giving, because if I'm stewarding God's money, He is holding me accountable for that. Tracy and I were sad because we knew the children in those orphanages needed the help. But I believe God wants our giving to be about more than just the stories. There needs to be accountability, stewardship, and good fruit in and through the organization as they steward what God blesses them with, just as I have to do with my banks, subcontractors, and vendors.

I mentioned our experience to Justin, and he introduced me to his friend Rob Hoskins. Rob's father, Bob, founded a ministry, OneHope, devoted to providing God's Word to every child in the world—an amazing goal. In 2004, Rob had become president of OneHope. They had a great reputation for being best in class, very strategic and wise, and good stewards of their resources, so I began to ask Rob questions about giving.

The lesson for me was that my friends with the African orphanages were focused on their responsibility to steward the orphanages, but their strengths were not in financial stewardship. The flip side of that is we can focus too much on our profits and neglect the people God puts in front of us. We have to find a balance so that we continue to make a profit so we can reach people for Christ and give to His kingdom.

Over the next two years, Rob helped me find that balance. He became one of my wise counselors and friends, helping me take the ideas I felt God was stirring in my spirit and commit them to prayer and then paper in a form that would allow us to execute and measure them.

In all the time that Rob was helping me build my vision, he never asked me for a donation to OneHope.

"I don't get it," I told him one day. "I've never worked with a leader of a nonprofit who invested so much in me. You've helped us with biblical knowledge and understanding, leadership, and our giving strategy. You've helped me think a different way. I don't even understand why you would do that. And you've never asked me for a dollar."

"Well, God didn't tell me to ask people for money," he said. "God told me to get the Word of God to every child in the world."

"Sure," I said, "but you still have bills to pay."

"We do, and we still have a lot to do. But we've learned over the years that God always gives us what we need. So, if I'm just loving God and serving people, God always provides."

God was teaching me through Justin and Rob how to love and how to give so that He could work more effectively through us. Our friends at the orphanage have something to learn through this experience, and so do I.

INTO THE
DESERT

Within a year after we started building in Harmony, the real estate market began to collapse. When I say collapse, I mean we were headed into the worst housing market in US history. We were beginning a time when we learned to rely more and more on the Lord because the crushing economic conditions were beyond anything we could manage.

Every morning I prayed for wisdom and for God's guidance in the decisions I needed to make that day. And I asked God to continue to touch the hearts of others, to guide them our way as we built communities.

We were still paying back our investors and reporting quarterly to them, and some quarters were not as good as others. I had to tell them, "We're doing the best we can." I would also tell them about plans and adjustments we were making so they weren't left wondering. I never tried to get out of those conversations, even when I knew they would be difficult and uncomfortable. Although no one liked these discussions, all of us continued to seek the Lord and trust Him even in these difficult times.

In fact, we took care of those who invested in us before we took care of ourselves. To do that, we remained lean as a company and a family. Profits were low, but we still managed to save a little for unexpected opportunities. In every opportunity, it was critical that we pray and seek the Lord on His will and follow His direction.

One of those opportunities came along in January 2008, when the parent company of Newmark Homes, one of the biggest builders in Texas, declared bankruptcy. Newmark was doing fine in our state but was having problems in Florida, where the parent company had 40 percent of its business. Florida was plummeting and taking the whole company, including the Texas division, down with it. The debt restructuring forced Newmark to release its lots in Harmony, and by then we were in a strong enough cash position to be a buyer, at a significant discount. We didn't buy their larger lots, which would have called for larger homes to be built on them. We stayed in our lane and focused on what we believed God was telling us to do—build smaller homes—without worrying about what everybody else was doing.

Our banker recognized our success and increased our line of credit to $7 million, which allowed us to build more homes and accept an opportunity in another development in nearby Garden Valley.

As the housing industry continued its collapse across the country, the US Treasury Secretary Henry Paulson warned, "The housing decline is . . . the most significant current risk to our economy."

The most significant current risk to the economy was the business I had chosen! And even though Texas had not been a big part of the boom years, I was about to feel the consequences of the nationwide collapse.

Banks all over the country were failing because they were overexposed to bad real estate deals. Many of the banks that remained open were cutting real estate from their lending portfolios as fast as they could. Our bank, Southwest Securities, was in that second group.

Our banker and friend, Alicia Bland, called me one morning in 2008. "I need to talk to you," she said, and I could tell by her voice it was serious.

"Okay," I said. "What is it?"

They were not going to be able to lend us any more money, she said, and I would have to find another bank.

Alicia knew we had been conservative in our borrowing from the beginning. We had never missed a payment, and we were selling some homes. The decision was not hers.

"It gets worse," she continued.

The bank was not immediately calling in our loan (they knew that would force us into bankruptcy), but I had to give them an aggressive repayment plan. How fast could we pay back our $7 million line of credit?

I didn't know. Seven million dollars. We had more than thirty homes under construction. We were closing three or four a month, but we needed access to cash to continue building.

I hung up and just sat in my chair. This could be the end of the company. We had a staff of about twenty people who would all lose their income if we were forced to shut down. We didn't have a chief financial officer I could talk to. This was my problem.

I left the office and drove home to pray. I had a God-size problem.

God, how are we going to do this? I prayed over and over.

"Trust Me," He said. "Trust Me."

The more I prayed, the more He reminded me to rely on Him.

I put my faith in the Lord, and I sensed His peace, but I also knew we had a lot of work to do. Our currency says, "In God We Trust," but the bank would not accept "Trust God" as our repayment plan. So, for the next two weeks, I analyzed every aspect of the company, looking into every corner of our financial spreadsheets, every supplier, every contractor, and every employee.

I prayed every morning for God to guide my thinking. Early on, He told me, "Don't gripe or complain about your situation. You're here for a reason. Stay the course. Focus on Me every day. Remember what I tell you."

I dug deeper into the numbers, and at the same time I was reaching out to other banks that might work with us and was coming up empty. Every bank was afraid to extend more money to builders—especially a relatively new builder whose line of credit was being frozen and called in by another bank. At that point, the best we could offer Southwest Securities was a two-year repayment plan.

I took that plan to Alicia, and her board agreed to accept it.

I was still not taking a salary, and our senior management team agreed to take cuts to keep from eliminating staff.

God continually reminded us of the biblical exodus story, the forty-year journey from Egypt to the promised land. Every day in the wilderness, God fed the Israelites just enough for each day.

Lord, give us today our daily bread. We need You and Your help; I don't even know what I'm doing, I prayed.

We had to change the way we did business even more by operating on cash and being tighter in our spending. We did the best we could to count the cost of every decision we made, including every board and every nail before we signed a contract. Every sale had to generate positive cash flow. And God did not give us a holiday on our tithe. I had been clear with Alicia that we would joyfully continue to tithe and give offerings on our profits to the kingdom, and the bank was okay with that, as long as we continued to address the loan. Honestly, I had to work to remain joyful and thankful in our giving, because my flesh was weak, but my spirit seemed to get stronger as we continued being faithful.

Every month I drove to the bank with a check. Sometimes I had to apologize. "This is all we can pay this month, but we're closing on more homes next month."

We slowly chipped away at our debt and stayed in regular, honest communication. Some months I thought I might have to turn a house over to the bank, but they never demanded or asked us to stop tithing or giving our offering. They knew we were working hard, doing our best, and being transparent. They may have been privately nervous about our ability to pull through, but they told me they trusted and understood. I truly believe the Lord was with us, guiding us, and giving His favor.

MY LACK OF
TRUST IN GOD

*D*espite the Lord's grace and compassion as He guided us through our most difficult financial time, I did not trust Him completely. Because of my incomplete trust, I made a terrible, undisciplined decision.

A customer came into our model home and told Rob Poole that he liked our homes, and he wondered if we would build a custom home for him on the lake. We'd never done that, and Rob was uncomfortable with the idea. I agreed with Rob, and I brushed the guy off. But the customer persisted, so I told Rob to get the information together. Then I sat down with the numbers and did the math and realized we could make about $200,000 on the house, enough to make a signif-icant impact on our profits for the year—remember, we were in the worst housing market in US history.

This was huge—like a gift from God. Except I didn't ask God if it was from Him. I didn't seek His guidance. I didn't even ask Rob, one of my most trusted counsels on our team.

Instead, I told Rob to call the guy and agree to build his house.

I made two mistakes in that decision. First, when I started the business, God had told me that my purpose was to reach people for Christ and give to the kingdom. Building houses was what I did. It was the vehicle, but it was not who I was, and it was not my purpose. Now, I was thinking only about the money and the bad market, and that should have been a red flag for me. I was acting out of fear, unsure of what the future held for us as recession clouds grew larger on the horizon.

Second, although I had an uneasy feeling in my spirit, I didn't slow down to pray about it or pray with Rob about the decision. I'm sure he would have at least stepped on the brakes if we had prayed together and heard what the Holy Spirit was telling us.

When we began construction, we experienced one problem after another. For example, the customer wanted a virtual glass wall overlooking the lake. But with the wind out there, we needed to add structure to give it enough strength. The customer didn't want that. He wanted much more expensive glass and larger panes. Our mistake. Then he wanted spray foam insulation, and our spray foam contractor and I were concerned about mold because the house was so close to the lake. We wanted to use a certain kind of foam, but he was adamant about wanting a different type that we didn't believe was the right one, and he wanted us to warranty it. He also wanted us to upgrade the floor tile to a product that was less durable and then to warranty that. He wanted a boat ramp, which we had never done. It was one thing after another, and the delays and money added up as we neared completion.

By the time we finished the project, we had spent so much extra time, hired engineers to confirm our work and protect us and the customer, and given in on so many issues that were not in the contract, we had actually lost money on the deal. We had not reached that customer for Christ, and we had no profit to give to the kingdom. In fact, we lost profits, causing us to reach fewer people for Christ and give less to the kingdom.

Years later, I said something to Rob about that project, and he said he'd felt uncomfortable about it from the beginning. If only . . .

If only I had prayerfully sought God's wisdom.

If only I had consulted Rob for his wise counsel and asked him to pray with me.

If only I had put aside my fear and greed, we never would have started that project.

I had built the wrong house for the wrong customer for the wrong reason. I had not trusted God to fulfill His promise to provide, and I had tried to provide for myself. I had allowed fear and doubt to entangle my mind and heart. I needed to study the Word of God, mediate on it day and night, and do what it said instead of losing focus. Lesson learned, I hoped.

This was all part of our exodus story—our time in the desert. I had prayed for God to feed us, and He had fed us. He had given us everything we needed. Then I became impatient, trying to provide extra manna for my own protection instead of trusting my true provider and protector.

As I think back on this story, I am humbled and reminded of what a great loving, merciful, and gracious God we serve. Jesus allows us to miss His blessing and do our own thing at times but does not condemn us. He allows us to learn, grow, and see Him in a way we may not have seen Him before. I have heard it said that our past is only a story unless we reflect on it with Jesus's perspective and learn from it what He wants to teach us. Then it becomes wisdom.

BEARING
HEALTHIER FRUIT

*E*ven as we were living through the real estate crisis, and even as we were reaching people for Christ and giving to kingdom work, God was working on other areas of my heart and spirit, often bringing the right people into my life at just the right time, like when I needed encouragement to be more self-disciplined with my personal health.

Every time I looked in the mirror, I could see years of too much ice cream and donuts and not enough self-discipline and exercise. I tried diets, sometimes the latest fad, but I didn't stick with them over the long haul. Our company was growing, and the daily routine there, on top of trying to be a good husband and father, always seemed to take priority over my personal health.

I hadn't been on a scale in years. That's how it happens. You take your eye off some area of your life, and the discipline and self-control slip away day by day. In this case, I had gained just a few pounds a year—a little bit at a time. Then the Lord began to ask me, "What kind of fruit do you want to bear?"

When I saw my reflection from the corner of my eye, He showed me the fruit of my lack of proper diet and exercise and began to reveal to me how that lack of self-control in my physical health was a reflection of my spiritual life.

"If you want to bear healthier fruit," the Lord said, "you have to make healthier choices."

There are a lot of reasons why people are over-weight, so please know that for me this had nothing to do with a health-related issue. For me, it was simple: my desire to enjoy tasty things was stronger than my desire to choose what was healthy. I was eating too much of the wrong foods. As far as exercise went, I had convinced myself that I didn't have time.

But the Lord didn't let up, and I began to explore through prayer and Scripture what He was saying.

As time passed, He told me, "Son, I love you, but if you can't control even the little things that you put in your mouth, how can I trust you to control bigger things?"

This was frustrating to me. Tracy and I were fully committed to the Lord. Why would He care if I was a few pounds overweight? I thought, *Does He not see all I do for Him, my prayer time, my Bible study time, serving the church, reaching people for Christ and giving to His kingdom?* Then, as I spent more time praying for His direction, He let me know this wasn't about what I did but about an intensive work in my spiritual discipline. This was about Him wanting to use me more. But I had to decrease (physically and spiritually) so I could have more of Him. He wasn't going to take away what He had given me, but He wasn't going to give me more to steward until I became self-controlled in my eating and exercise.

My diet was a symptom of other issues I needed to address. God was talking to me about my whole life. In time He would reveal those deeper issues. For now, I would take the first step, which was to join a fitness center. I finally stepped onto a scale and discovered I was about sixty-five pounds overweight. One of the trainers there, Troy Grant, set me up in the cardio room and then on the weight machines. Then he explained that to lose sixty-five pounds in a year, which was my goal, I had to burn five hundred more calories than I consumed every day. He told me that working out was important, but 85 percent of weight loss was what I put in my mouth. My family ate a lot of Mexican food, and I started eating chicken with no oil or butter, and charro beans with no juice or tortillas. At times, I ate the same thing ten meals a week. Sounds crazy, right? My family thought so too.

Still, it was hard for me because I was so badly out of shape and struggling to stick with a workout routine. Troy left the fitness center to start his own company, and that turned out to be great for me. I went with him to a different gym, and for a while I was one of his only clients. I needed the extra time and encouragement.

Then one day Jason Dodson stepped into my office. He had been working for us from almost our first day—he was my sixth hire. Jason didn't have a professional background in construction (he had been in insurance previously), but his family had been in the business, and he was a natural. He had discipline, paid attention to detail, and had an understanding of construction.

After he took over construction for us at Harmony, I never saw him without a stack of spreadsheets in a binder or folder. Jason didn't trust his memory to keep up with all the subs in all the houses. With all those spreadsheets, he saw at a glance what was happening tomorrow, next week, and several weeks out on every house. If we had a delay, he could immediately plug that in and see the impact all the way through.

Jason may have perceived my own need for more discipline and structure to meet my fitness goals, though he never would have said so. We had become friends, and I think God laid it on his heart to reach out to me. Whatever his motivation, he offered to meet me at the gym early in the morning, five days a week, for a year.

This was an incredible offer and sacrifice for Jason to meet me at 6 a.m., because I knew he was not a morning person. We were there an hour before sunrise, day after day, month after month. Hardly anybody likes getting up that early. Now, he was doing it not for himself, but for me. Going forward, I would be accountable to the Lord, a trainer, and to Jason (I needed a lot of help).

The morning workouts quickly became more than just exercise for me. I would get to the gym thirty minutes before the guys and spent that time working on cardio. As I exercised, I listened to the Bible, starting with a chapter from Proverbs that aligned with the day of the month (Proverbs 1 on the first, and so on). Then I listened to a chapter from another book in the Bible. I was praying as I listened, so it was like having a conversation with God—not aloud but in my mind and heart, paying attention to what I was listening to and thanking Jesus. I prayed on many mornings, asking God to give me strength, energy, and perseverance to stay faithful to what He had asked me to do. I would then ask, *Lord, what do You want to say to me today?* Often a verse I had just listened to might pop up in my mind and spirit, and I would text myself a note from my phone to study, pray about, and meditate on it that day.

After cardio, Jason and I would be talking while we worked through the weight machines. He was a deeply committed Christian, and we often discussed what we felt God was speaking to us.

For the entire year, with Troy as my guide and Jason as my encourager, I kept my early morning appointments at the gym, with the Lord speaking in His still small voice through His Word and my friend.

God was using this discipline to transform my body, my mind, and my spirit. Instead of lying in bed, I was listening to His Word. After twelve months, I had lost sixty-five pounds, and I had grown in Him and with Jason. Jesus showed me that if I addressed my health with intentionality, discipline, and self-control, then I would gain fruit from it, and I did. I lost weight, became healthier, and had more energy. More importantly, I learned that my spirit is the same as my physical body in this way: What I feed my physical body gains either fat or healthy muscle. Likewise, if I take in unhealthy spiritual things, then little by little I become spiritually fat and unhealthy.

That workout/listening time has become an established habit that God uses in multiple ways to teach me about stewarding my health, my finances, and my relationships, as I realize the little decisions I make have big implications and determine the fruit I bear.

SEVEN
DOORS OPEN

*F*inally, a few years after our banker told us to repay our $7 million line of credit, we made our last payment. But once we did, we had little cash on hand. Credit lines were still very hard to get because of the housing recession, and it seemed we were in no position to grow the company.

Then, out of the blue, a guy called me and said, "You don't know me, but I was on the board of directors at Southwest Securities."

He had recently moved to a different bank, and he said, "I watched how you managed your business and communicated with the bank, and I'm wondering if you might want to talk with us about a line of credit."

Well, of course we would.

Over the next year, I got six more calls like that from bankers who had seen what we had done and wanted to offer credit for us to build homes. Seven banks offered us credit lines for construction totaling $35 million. God is so good. He had led us, directed our steps, and fed us day by day while teaching us to trust Him more, to be more disciplined, to count the cost of our decisions even more, and now He was giving us access to the resources that would take our company to a new level.

These lines of credit opened new opportunities to go to developers whose builders were literally walking away from them. During this time, the Lord reminded us of our mission: "I have opened these doors so you can reach people by loving them and serving them." As we prayed, the Lord began to show us that developers were hurting and that we could help serve them and the banks. We did this by telling developers we would put a model home and two spec houses in their subdivisions. We would continue to keep two specs under construction as we sold homes, but we also had to steward resources well. We asked them to allow us to have first right of refusal on every remaining lot in the subdivision, even if they were not developed. The arrangement was a win for developers and allowed us to be ready when the economy improved.

WHEN THE ONLY
HOPE WAS PRAYER

*B*obby Glass was a successful developer who, like so many others, was struggling. Bobby believed Jesus's promise, "Where two or three gather in my name, there am I with them" (Matthew 18:20), and called me at my office and asked if I would pray with him.

I didn't know Bobby, but I knew his reputation. His father had played football at Baylor and then in the NFL, had led locker room Bible studies in the early 1960s, and later founded an evangelical prison ministry, taking his Christian witness "behind the walls." Bobby had followed his father's footsteps in many ways, including as an all-conference offensive lineman at Baylor before starting his development company. My own company was just a few years old, and I hadn't yet built in any of his subdivisions.

When Bobby called me, he said he'd heard I was a praying man and wondered if I would meet him at his Shiloh Forest development. I told him I would.

Shiloh Forest was like hundreds, maybe thousands, of other residential developments across the country—paved streets, a few houses completed, a few more under construction, and acres of empty lots. Developers like Bobby had invested millions of dollars installing the infrastructure when the market was expanding, counting on the income from lot sales to repay loans and lines of credit. Then the market collapsed in places like Florida and Las Vegas, and the dominoes fell all over the place. Huge national developers experienced losses in other areas of the country and felt the ripples all the way to Texas. Bankers here pulled back from commitments out of fear and/or their own financial struggles, leaving large builders and developers without access to the cash they needed to finish projects.

Bobby was already at Shiloh Forest when I drove up. I climbed out of my pickup and into his, and we drove through the development talking about the business for a few minutes. But we were there to pray, so Bobby parked the truck and we prayed.

We expressed to God that neither of us understood what was going on. *But You are God, and You can do whatever You want*, I prayed. *So, if it's Your will for Bobby and his company to get out of this struggle they're in, then give them thoughts, ideas, and creativity. Give them peace, endurance, and the strength they need. Remind them how much You love them and care about them above all else.*

Then several important things happened in that truck. For perhaps the first time, I began to understand how big this recession was—and was going to be—as well as how many great men and women of God were being impacted along with us. Only God could help us. Bobby had been praying for months, and so had his family. He already knew he could not manage the impact of the downturn on his own. *Lord, I need help*, he had prayed.

I had prayed for God's help before, but not the way Bobby was praying. Here was a man who had been developing property for way longer than I had been building houses. His father was an evangelist, and his parents had created a loving home for him to grow up in. Yet he reached out to me, a virtual stranger but brother in Christ, to pray with him.

We finished praying, and I didn't know how God might answer our prayers. I couldn't afford to pay Bobby's loans or do something miraculous like that, but I could come alongside him and continue to offer prayer.

A few days later, I felt God telling me that He wanted us to build homes in Bobby's development, and He gave me an idea. Bobby and I were using the same bank, and the Federal Reserve was limiting how much the banks could lend for real estate. In this case, though, lending money to my company to buy a few of Bobby's lots cleaned those troubled assets off the bank's books. I could build houses on those lots, get those lots off Bobby's books and the bank's books, and everybody would win.

We were taking some risk by building spec houses on the Shiloh Forest lots, but we didn't build so many that we got ahead of the market. Plus, I really sensed Jesus asking us to do this for His glory. We put down some earnest money on about a hundred lots and then built and sold the homes until we had worked through the whole development. So everybody won—Bobby, the bank, home buyers, us, and, most importantly, Jesus who still gets all the glory. I believe that's what God had in mind when He nudged Bobby to invite me to pray with him and allowed us both to be part of this God story.

That was an important lesson from my relationship with Bobby Glass. Bobby had grown up surrounded by prayer, and his parents were still praying for him every day, as were his wife and family. He was a committed Christian. Still, he came to a place where he needed even more help—more people praying with him and for him. I learned that sometimes we have to reach out and share our needs and our fears with others, sometimes even with strangers.

Prayer enables God to move us. In this situation, through Bobby's prayers, God touched my heart and led me to a place where He could help Bobby through us and the company. That was my purpose here. And it turned out to be a great opportunity. Over time, we bought virtually all of the remaining lots, and we've built in more of Bobby's developments since then. God asked me to be available, to pray with Bobby, and to do what I could to help. Then He created opportunities none of us had considered.

WHO IS MY CUSTOMER?

One of the most loved of Jesus's parables, the parable of the good Samaritan, pivots on the question, "Who is my neighbor?" (Luke 10:29).

We were building at Shiloh Forest when God challenged me with a question: "Who is your customer?"

Our customers were the home buyers, of course.

"No," I felt the Lord telling me. "Not anymore. Your thinking is too limited."

Then He began to open my eyes to a new way of seeing "customers" as more than just the people buying homes from us. God had called us to reach people for Christ and give to the kingdom. The vehicle He gave us to do this was building and selling homes. But what would we do when home sales slowed? How would we serve?

I shared with our team what I was hearing from the Lord, and we prayerfully analyzed all of our business relationships. God led us to think of ourselves serving developers, bankers, vendors, and everybody else we worked with differently, treating them like customers and seeking opportunities to serve them so they could be more successful.

A win for them could mean a win for us but most importantly for the kingdom of God. Business does not have to be a zero-sum game.

It wasn't long before God gave us an opportunity to put this idea into action. A neighbor and I were sharing some of the struggles we were facing in the industry. He worked for another builder, and as we talked, God laid that builder on my heart. I asked if I could come to a nearby subdivision, where the developer was struggling to sell enough homes to stay in business, and pray with him. We met in his model home, encouraged one another, and prayed, trusting the Lord's will to be done.

This time I didn't have money to buy more lots, and the Lord wasn't asking me to. I was there just to pray. A year and a half later, though, the bank took back the property, and everybody was going to end up losing. I talked with our team about the situation, and we prayed together, asking God if there might be an opportunity for us to participate in a way that would lead to success for everybody involved.

We created a plan similar to what had worked at Shiloh Forest. The bank agreed to let us buy the lots they now owned and the future undeveloped dirt on the property, and we would use most of the profits from each house we sold to pay down the note. We were able to replicate that plan in other places, helping other banks get the debt off their books faster.

We were also helping other developers by buying the property for the debt owed and keeping what would have been negative balances off their credit lines. They still lost the money they had already invested, but they could continue their business without the burden of that additional debt to the bank. We were buying the property, and we saw that as a win for all of us.

In another situation, a builder was struggling to finish ten or twelve houses because of issues with his banker. We were able to step in and help him finish the houses so he could get them sold. We received money to cover our costs, but more importantly, the builder and the bank came out without losses. Subcontractors and suppliers were able to fulfill their commitments and get paid, and we came away with more strong relationships.

I'm not suggesting we should intentionally do things that would lose money and put our business at risk. That's not good stewardship. But generous love says, "If I can help you make that work, and I've got the staff, the resources, and the time, then of course, we'll help you do it."

All along, God continued to remind us that we serve Him and then we serve people. Sometimes that service is going to be more profitable, sometimes not.

At the time that we were acquiring lots in Shiloh Forest and this nearby subdivision, we didn't understand everything that was happening from God's perspective. I see now that God was taking care of those developers and bankers while He was taking care of us and showing us that if we love Him and we love and serve others, He will bless us above anything we might hope for.

We also knew that our long-term vision required us to have more lots. We needed more relationships with bankers and developers. We expanded our business when others in our industry were not. We didn't have to make a lot of money to build our value long term.

The Lord led us to make decisions contrary to what other builders and developers were doing and even the direction the economy was heading. When the rest of the world was retreating, God was telling us to advance. We were going after more lots, buying as many as we could buy, but God was doing it His way—not the way our finite minds would have done it but the way the infinite God would.

Over time, our aggressive buying actually hurt our reputation among other builders. They thought we were trying to control all the land and put them out of business, and that bothered me deeply. God had called me to reach people for Christ, not hurt them. So how could I be effective if they thought we were trying to undermine them?

In response, still during the recession, the Lord told us to do two things that reinforced our new idea of customers. First, start selling lots to other builders to create relationships with them. You see, builders generally don't sell lots to other builders; other than our people, land is one of a builder's greatest assets. If we sell a lot, that's one less potential home we can build and sell—and one more our competitor can. God showed us that if we *do* sell a lot, then we can build a relationship and have an opportunity to share the hope that is within us.

Second, God said He wanted us to start a development company. Again, He wanted us to create relationships with other builders—our competitors in the world's eyes—through development. This was another way God was telling us to reach people for Christ and give to His kingdom. I thought it was about building and selling homes, but I had to get God's perspective, not my little perspective that the customer was the person buying the home. He was showing me that these companies are vehicles for relational evangelism, loving people where they are and serving them by helping meet their needs according to His riches and glory.

However, at the time it was also really making us have to trust in Him even more. Developers across the country were pulling back or shutting down altogether. How could we expect to do any better than they were?

I had never done any work as a developer and didn't know anything about it. But I knew a guy who did, Terry Weaver. He was already moving toward retirement, and he could get us started in the business. He wouldn't be working with us for decades, but Terry had the heart and the skill set we needed to reach people for Christ and give to the kingdom through building the business.

We followed God's leading, and He used the Great Recession to transform our homebuilding company, start a development company, and create opportunities for strong, positive relationships with people, from bankers, to developers, to builders, to home buyers, and more. I had hoped Terry would stay for three years, but instead he guided our development company for five.

As the recession wore on, opportunities increased because even more large, publicly traded home-builders and developers went on the defensive and stopped buying land. Unable to sell enough homes to maintain their quarterly profits, they looked for ways to mitigate the huge losses they were taking. One mitigation strategy was to sell as many lots as possible for whatever they could get for them. Flooding the market with lots drove prices down for all the developers, forcing more of them to sell into the downward spiral. Some smaller developers looked for opportunities to retire and liquidate their holdings altogether. By the end of the recession, we owned or controlled about 8,600 lots, which was crazy.

God continued to stress that we not buy lots at predatory prices. He didn't want us to work a win-lose strategy, where we won and the sellers lost. They belong to God, just as our company belongs to God. He wanted us to continue building strong relationships with other developers, treating them like customers, as we grew our companies, and I believe we did the best we knew at the time. One of the most interesting things about this season, as I reflect on it, is that I see God all over it. But in the midst of it, I was simply trying to seek the Lord and follow Him step-by-step.

Our success did not come from great business abilities or amazing strategies on our part. It was simply a result of Jesus being with us and going before us. He allowed us to walk through many hard times, and I know there will be more. Through these times, He always reminds us to study the Word of God, mediate on it day and night, do what it says; then you will be prosperous and successful in all your ways (Joshua 1:8). It is a journey with Jesus, not a destination to get to Him.

I am also reminded that many great men and women of God did not come out of that recession as we did, even though they stayed faithful to the Lord. I don't always understand God's ways or His thoughts, but He does, and I can trust that. God makes the way and orders our steps for a closer relationship with Him for His glory.

GOD WAS MY HEADHUNTER

*T*o succeed in the direction God had given us— buying more lots and starting a development company in the middle of the real estate collapse—I needed to surround myself with people who had different gifts and talents than mine. But I honestly did not know exactly what I needed.

Then one Sunday, our senior pastor, Scott Wilson, was preaching a message and asked us to pray that God would bring people to do God's work in the church. His request resonated with me, and that afternoon at home, I prayed that prayer for our church. In response, I felt God saying, "Why aren't you asking Me to bring people to your business to do My work?"

Great question! I thought. Maybe He would be the source of the expertise we needed. He knew far better than I did what we needed to do His work. After all, He'd been my ultimate Matchmaker.

When I was single, lonely, and wanted a family, I had asked God to help me, and He brought Tracy Miller into my life. Her family became an incredibly positive influence even before we were married. Tracy became my wife, my life partner, my prayer partner, and my business partner. God had answered that prayer in ways I had never imagined. Through Scott's message and my prayers, I believed He was telling me that He could do that for our company—bring the right people to our work.

My prayers were for people to help build the company and join us in kingdom work, and God answered with people who would also build change in me. In fact, He had started sending the people before I began asking Him, before I even founded the company.

I had an undergraduate business degree, and before I started our homebuilding company, I worked for seven and a half years with the Annuity Board of the Southern Baptist Convention. I had a good enough understanding of finance to lead our mom-and-pop-size operation, but the Lord had given me a vision of a much larger and financially complex company. I didn't have the knowledge and experience I needed to build a strategy and financial plan for where I believed God wanted us to go. I had the vision, but I needed the Lord to bring the right people with the right gifts to help us achieve our mission and grow the business.

In 2008, in the middle of the housing crash, we needed to hire a chief financial officer, but we didn't have money to pay for that expertise.

God was on it. He had been on it for three years. But I wouldn't learn the whole story until years later.

In 2005, a guest minister visited a church 1,500 miles away in Montclair, New Jersey, and spoke to a man I had never met. At the end of the service the guest minister pulled Terry Trayvick and his wife, Sandy, aside from the crowd and said he had a prophetic word for them: "Your work environment is about to change, and what seems like a demotion to you will be a kingdom promotion."

Of course, Terry and Sandy didn't know what the man was talking about. A "demotion" made no sense. Anybody looking at Terry's résumé would have said he was a superstar in business. After succeeding with Sarah Lee, General Motors, and Proctor & Gamble, he joined another Fortune 500 company, R. R. Donnelley & Sons, when he was thirty-five years old. Within five years at Donnelley, he was tapped to lead the company's capital market business, and two years later, he was named president of the book manufacturing division, with more than five thousand employees. As president, Terry was given what they call a "golden parachute," which meant that if the company ever asked him to leave, they would pay him a significant lump sum amount. He hardly even looked at the agreement because he had no intention of leaving.

Then he heard the prophecy, and the next day at work, Terry could feel the ground underneath him shifting. Soon after that, his boss said the company was restructuring, and they wanted Terry to move to Chicago and run corporate strategy. Professionally, the shift would be right in Terry's wheelhouse. He had cut his teeth running strategy, transforming troubled business units into successful ones. But personally, a move from New Jersey to Chicago was a problem. He and Sandy had three children (one with special needs), and a move would be terribly disruptive. Plus, they were extremely involved in their church and didn't want to leave that community.

Terry asked what would happen if he declined the opportunity.

He was told he had only two choices: accept the new position or leave the company and take the golden parachute agreement.

Terry knew instantly that God was in control. He was just hitting his prime at forty-three years old, and God was about to open new doors.

Maybe another company would reach out to him. A friend, another corporate president, had told him that once you become a president of a major corporation, it's almost like being an NBA coach. You can get fired four or five times, but somebody is always going to pick you up. That wasn't what Terry wanted.

That night he and Sandy prayed for a long time, seeking to understand what God wanted them to do, and it became clear to them that He wanted Terry to leave the corporate world, at least for a season. Beyond that, Terry saw no plan. He had no time to develop a strategy for himself. Just leave and trust the Lord.

He knew that he could use the golden parachute agreement to cover the family's living expenses while they waited for God to reveal their next step. He declined the move to Chicago, then Donnelley dismissed him and wrote him a check. He offered his skills to his pastor and church, and they asked him to serve as chief of staff. While serving in that role, Terry saw Christian businessmen who needed the kind of expertise and wisdom he could offer as a consultant, and he began to visualize a role for himself. Around the same time, God gave Terry a vision, saying, "Every hour of every day in every country, someone will be helped as a result of what I'm going to do through you."

Two years later, God started working on my side of the equation, stirring my spirit and asking me to trust Him. I had no idea He was bringing Terry and me together.

Our church was growing fast, and Pastor Scott Wilson and church leaders wanted to add a television ministry. To help make that happen, Scott hired Kelvin Co, a young man who was running media programming for a megachurch in New Jersey. Kelvin and his family moved to Texas, and we built a house for them.

Scott also had a heart for business leaders, and he had created a leadership forum, inviting speakers to come to our church every month and share leadership principles with businesspeople. A few months after Kelvin joined the staff, Scott asked him what he thought of the forum.

"I think it's fabulous," Kelvin replied, "except that we promised to bless them with business leadership. So far, I've only heard pastors, and when I look back at the library of recordings, all of those speakers were pastors."

"You're right," Scott said. "Who would you recommend to speak?"

Kelvin told him about his former boss at Christ Church back in New Jersey, Terry Trayvick, a successful businessman who was following God with all his heart. Scott agreed to invite Terry out to speak.

Kelvin called me to make sure I would be there the night Terry spoke, because he believed our hearts and vision were closely aligned. At the forum, Terry told some of his personal story, and he talked about the importance of developing strategy in business, advising us to ask ourselves three questions:

- How are we going to grow the business?
- How are we going to become more efficient?
- How are we going to distinguish ourselves from our competitors?

Growth, efficiency, and distinctiveness, he said, are pillars of success for a company.

This was exactly what I needed! When he finished speaking, I practically raced to the front of the room to meet him. As we talked, I became even more convinced that Terry's business expertise could help us take our company to a whole new level.

I needed help creating a strategic plan to execute the vision the Lord had given us—to organize it and create a system that people could follow to transform the vision into reality. That was Terry's gift. But we didn't have money to pay him.

In the short term, I needed a chief financial officer. We didn't have money to pay him for that either. I told Terry that, yet he was willing to meet with me anyway.

He came back to Texas, and when he walked into the office that morning, he looked like he had come straight from Wall Street, wearing a perfectly tailored three-button suit. I wore a T-shirt and jeans. I almost always wear a T-shirt and jeans.

We got to work, with Terry asking a lot of questions through the morning. He was intrigued by our vision to reach people for Christ and give to the kingdom through a homebuilding company. The process of marketing, building, and selling homes created dozens of opportunities to connect with people.

Late in the morning we took a break to get lunch. Walking to the truck I remembered I had a deer in the back. I had gone hunting that morning and had killed a nice buck, and I was going to get it mounted.

I told Terry, "I need to go to the taxidermist on the way."

"Sure," he said. We got in the truck and talked business a little longer, and I pulled into a driveway to a small building. The taxidermist was in back.

"Can you help me get this deer out of the back?" I asked.

"What?" Terry exclaimed. "Oh, I thought you said you were going to see your tax accountant!"

We laughed, and we must have been a sight, a five-foot-seven White man in a T-shirt and jeans and a six-foot-five Black man in a sharp business suit dragging a dead deer across a gravel driveway. Terry turned to me with a smile and said, "You know, we really come from two different worlds, one big New York City guy and the other a country boy. Only Christ could have brought us together."

After a couple of days working together, I knew we needed Terry's help day to day in a big way but had no idea how that could ever happen. Just before Terry left, we decided we could not afford to hire him but could pay him a little to consult and help us get a strategic plan started and help me think through our finances, which he had already been digging into. He wouldn't have to move to Texas; he could oversee our finances from New Jersey and fly out occasionally for meetings. I really wanted to hire him as our CFO, but we literally didn't have the money to pay him. So I tried to put that idea out of my mind, and Terry returned home.

In my prayer time God kept telling me, "Ask him. Ask him." But I thought it was just my own desire.

Then one Saturday morning, Tracy told me that God had spoken to her during her prayer time saying He wanted Terry to come to work with us. It confirmed what the Lord had been laying on my heart, but I told her we had no money, and Terry knew it because he had seen our finances, so it would take a miracle.

Later the same morning, Terry called out of the blue, and we talked for a few minutes. Then he said, "Is there something you want to ask me?"

"Yes," I answered, "but it doesn't make any sense."

I told him that Tracy and I had felt the Lord telling each of us that I should ask Terry to come to work with me. "But you've seen our finances," I said. "You know we don't have money to pay you."

"That's interesting," he replied, "because Sandy and I felt God telling us in our prayer time that I'm supposed to reach back out to you and offer my help."

I felt an unbelievable rush of God's assurance. He was just waiting for me to ask!

I shared more details with Terry about what I thought God was telling me, that I needed someone with his heart for Jesus, his wisdom, and his strengths to be our chief financial officer. Before he answered, I had to remind him of our financial situation again— although he already knew.

I expected him to say, "Let me pray about it."

Instead, he assured me that God was telling him to join Tracy and me in our work. He and Sandy believed so strongly, they were willing for Terry to work for this startup company that might never have enough revenue to pay him.

In a commonsense world, Terry never would have offered to work for no pay until the Lord provided enough for us to pay him. He knew there was the possibility that he might never be paid, but he was okay with that because God had led him here.

"God already paid me," he said, referring to the contract payout from his previous job. "And we know He is going to provide."

Who does that? Who goes to work with no promise of future pay or even a future position?

Terry knew as well as I did that God had brought him to us. His yes was to God, not to me, and that was very humbling to me.

After six months, in large part because of Terry's guidance, we were making enough money to pay him.

GIVING GOD ALL
OF OUR CASH

*T*racy and I were sitting in church one Sunday morning in 2010 when I felt like God was saying, "I want you to give Me all your money."

I didn't understand at the time, but I was sure God was saying, "I really want you to trust Me in this. I'm not only asking you to give Me your tithe but I'm asking you to give all the cash you and Tracy have—not just in your personal account but everything in the business accounts as well."

We were building momentum financially during perilous times, and a little cash in the bank gave us a safety net. I processed things pretty fast—I don't need days or weeks on something like this—and despite all logic, I was confident that this was the Lord speaking to me.

I leaned over to Tracy and said quietly, "Hey, I really believe God is telling us that we need to give away all our money." She didn't say anything or tell me I was nuts, so I kept whispering. "Not just our personal money, but even the company money."

I had her attention now. Tracy hears God speaking to her, and she knows He speaks to me too. We trust each other to discern the truth He is speaking to us.

"If you believe that's what God is telling you to do," she said, "let's do it."

We walked out of church not knowing where God might be leading us, but we committed to praying together and separately to seek confirmation and clarification of what I had heard.

Emptying our bank accounts would expose us and the company to risks that could affect the families of everyone who was working for us. We didn't take this lightly but wanted to be faithful and obedient.

We tried to keep extra money in the bank to give us a buffer against slowing cash flow, and now God was telling us to empty our accounts.

We were one of the few builders that could get loans to build spec houses at that time, and we had several of those underway. If we didn't sell them by the time we finished them, we would be sitting on that debt, and the interest every month, until buyers came along.

Terry Trayvick joined Tracy and me in prayer, and after several days we all felt God confirming what He had told me in church. We had about $50,000 cash across several different accounts, and I have to admit

I was a little nervous as I signed checks to give it away. With a pen in my hand, I started praying, *Lord Jesus, I may not understand, but in faith we are stepping out and trusting You. As we do, please take care of our staff and all our needs according to Your will and Your way.*

In fact, God had already shown us His faithfulness over and over again in years past. But He had never asked us to do something like this.

By December 31, we had cleared out our accounts, and from January 1 up to March 15, 2011, we closed on a few houses and generated just enough cash to cover payroll and the company expenses. Praise God!

We had moved on and did not think again about giving that cash to the Lord. We never asked or expected Him to respond with the miraculous. We lived day by day learning more and more to trust the Lord to guide our steps and provide for our needs. That was not a new frame of mind for Tracy and me. We had lived in financial survival mode for many years through our marriage. But when mid-April rolled around, we faced a deadline to pay our corporate taxes for the previous year and to pay for some lots in a new subdivision we were going into—totaling $500,000 that we didn't have.

Now I was really feeling the pressure. I looked at the schedule of homes we were closing, and the numbers didn't add up. I didn't know where these funds would come from to provide for this real need.

That's when God stepped up. As I mentioned, we were one of the few companies building spec houses, and around the first of April several buyers showed up out of nowhere looking at homes. "We need to close as soon as possible," one couple said, "and we're paying cash."

Then a guy I had loaned money to a few years earlier (and I had forgotten) called and said, "Hey, I've got your money."

Over the first ten days of April, we sold spec houses like crazy and closed on a couple of contract houses ahead of schedule. Then on a Saturday morning Terry called me at home and said, "I've gone through the accounts multiple times, and there's money in there that I've never seen."

I asked him to check again, and he replied, "I'm in the system all the time."

Somehow God had provided the cash we needed to pay our taxes and close on the lots in a matter of weeks.

God, how did You do that? I asked. The whole thing was nuts.

Then God spoke to me and said, "Son, this is how I work. You gave Me that $50,000 in December in advance of what I knew I was going to do in April. So for you, it was a step of faith. I knew what I was going to do, and I was just growing your faith." I was reminded of the story in Matthew 17:27, where Jesus provided the tax money out of a fish's mouth. He provided for us in miraculous ways as well.

As I write this story, I would never recommend people to do what we did unless God asks you to do it and you know it. But what I do know is that's what God asked us to do. And for me, He made something happen that I never could have done on my own. He was showing me His great love, grace, mercy, and faithfulness through finances, which had been one of my biggest weaknesses.

His mercy had sustained Tracy and me when we became so financially overextended early in our marriage that we had filed for bankruptcy. My parents had also filed for bankruptcy when I was a kid, and the two experiences made a lasting mark on me.

I struggled to hold on to every dollar because of my greed, but God was leading me to greater trust and cleansing my heart, allowing me to go even deeper in relationship with Him through circumstances like this one.

RADICAL
TRANSFORMATION

One morning God completely changed how I lived my life when He told me, "Son, My relationship with you is so important that you are going to have to set everything else aside. Your number one priority has to be your relationship with Me. I will never leave you, and I will take care of everything as you follow Me. Your number two relationship has to be with your wife. And number three has to be with your kids. And a lot of stuff in your life has to change for us to go where we're going."

The changes He was already leading me through certainly had an impact on my relationships, but this was different.

So, what would that look like?

More change, beginning with the way I prayed. When I prayed, I did the talking. That's the definition of prayer, right? You talk to God. Sometimes I stopped talking and listened, and I heard God speak to me through Scripture. But mostly I was telling God everything I was feeling and everything I needed. I might be praying for other people or for our church, but even in those cases, it was me talking and God listening.

I prayed about our business. I asked God for guidance in important decisions. The business grew, and we built more houses. We reached more people for Christ, and we gave more to His kingdom.

Then one day during my prayers, God said, "Slow down! Don't talk so much! Yes, your business is important to Me, and the decisions you make matter, but they're nowhere near as important to Me as you are. You're focused on how many people you can reach for Me and how much you can give to My kingdom. Our relationship is not a numbers game. It is not about what you do for Me but about our relationship with each other. Focus on *Me and let Me take care of everything else for now!*"

And that's how it started: my journey to know God better, to hear Him more, to know and experience His love in a real, personal way—one day, one issue, one step at a time.

As I listened, God gave me a vision of my heart, and I could see parts that were beating healthy and strong. But I could also see a lot of black spots. In my vision God said, "Those black spots represent sin, hardness of your heart, and other things that are not healthy. That is what I'm talking about. Over time, I'm going to show you what each one of those little dark spots represents in your life. I'm going to show you how to change each one of them and what to replace them with. And then I'm going to take out each of those spots and replace them with new tissue so that you no longer have a heart of stone. You can have a tender heart, bright and healthy."

He also told me that in this life, I will never be completely rid of the black spots. I will not arrive at the point where I can say, "Okay, now my heart is pure." If we think we can say that, we've missed God. If God did it any other way—if He completely purified our hearts in this life—we wouldn't remain dependent on Him. Our need for Him would go away, once we're convinced we've arrived. He never stops pursuing us, and He never wants us to forget that.

God was about to transform my heart. You see, for most of my life as a Christian, I had lived by His law, as expressed in the Bible. I tried to live by that law, and as a result I offered less grace and forgiveness. I wanted to be holy, for God says, "Be holy, because I am holy" (Leviticus 11:44). I wanted to be righteous, and I felt I knew where the lines between righteous and unrighteous were. I didn't want to cross those lines, so I sometimes drew three more lines in front of the real line to make sure I didn't even get close to it. That's where legalism came into play. Good-hearted parents say, "I am going to protect my kids" or "I want to protect people in the church, and we don't want them to get anywhere near lust issues. So let's make sure everybody dresses in a way that no one could be tempted and the devil could win—so stay far away from sin and sinners so you don't fall into temptation."

That's an exaggeration, of course, but that's where legalism can take us. That's where it had been taking me. I worried more about the rules than about loving people and reaching the lost.

Many of the adults in the church I attended while I was growing up had put their trust in the law, so that was the model I followed. I relied on the law to guide me as a husband, a father, and a businessman. I lacked genuine love, grace, mercy, and empathy for others: "Dude, pull your bootstraps up and get over yourself. Get over your sin. Just quit doing it. All you have to do is choose to stop sinning." Those weren't just my thoughts. Those were my actual words. I actually told people things like, "All you have to do is decide not to drink, and you won't be an alcoholic."

The first chapter in the book of Romans lists the characteristics of sinners, of unrighteous people, and

I tried to avoid those things. Like so many Christians, I look at that list and find it easier to judge people whose sins are different from mine.

When I saw other people committing sins that I did not regularly commit, I sometimes called them out. If I didn't do it verbally I would in my mind and heart, especially of the people closest to me. I believed that was my responsibility as a Christian living among other Christians, to help them grow closer to Jesus.

Then God allowed me to see myself more clearly. Not all at once, thankfully. As I wrote earlier, God's first step was to get me to address my lack of discipline and self-control as evidenced by my overweight body. He sent me to the gym and then spoke to me every morning as I listened to the Bible while I did cardio.

During those months I spent getting my weight under control with diet and exercise, feeling my undisciplined years in my burning lungs and pounding heart, my body grew stronger and more fit. And as I listened to God's Word during my exercise time, my heart softened a little bit right there in the gym. I knew the Lord's goal in this process was not that I have 8 percent body fat and a six-pack but rather that the physical changes reflected what was happening in my spirit—those spiritual muscles were being stretched and worked, becoming healthier and more usable.

Next, He showed me my lack of grace for other people. I had been slow to try to understand and slow to forgive. I had been like the Pharisee at the temple, who looked at the sinner beside him and prayed, "God, I thank you that I am not like other people—robbers, evildoers, adulterers—or even like this tax collector. I fast twice a week and give a tenth of all I get" (Luke 18:11–12).

In my prayer time, God said, "Son, stop looking at other people and thinking about what they're doing wrong."

He said, "Live by love, not by law. Son, you have so much sin in your life that I can't reveal it all to you at once because you couldn't handle it. But I also have so much love for you that I can't pour it all out on you at once."

Of all the things the Lord has spoken to me, this might have been the most important and most difficult for me to understand and internalize. I didn't know what He meant, and I didn't know what to do.

Our God is a good God who knows that my understanding comes slowly, so He gave concrete examples for me to see and understand. Here's one: During Tracy's final year of employment at JCPenney, long before working from home was a thing, she was allowed to do some of her work from home, which alleviated a lot of pressure on our family and our marriage. That experience softened my heart toward employees and their lives outside of the company.

We've learned some of the costs that the company incurs when we seek a healthy balance for our employees—for example, sometimes a project may take longer to complete. But we've also learned to anticipate the demands of a critical project in advance, and we can all schedule our time in a more balanced manner.

I'm writing this book many years later, and over that time, God has continually given me insights that have changed my heart.

The bottom line is this: I didn't know how to love because I didn't really know God's love for me, and I didn't know what I didn't know. My love was centered on myself. I wanted to love God and love people, but I also expected them to love me back. My love was transactional. Even with Tracy. I was taking care of her, providing for her, holding her when she was hurt, but I wasn't loving her where she needed to be loved.

Then God told me that I should focus first on my relationship with Him: "This is a conversation between you and Me. You have sin in your own life, issues that you need to address before I can take you any further."

Those words might have crushed me—if He had left me alone to address my sin—but then God opened my eyes to another verse:

> *In kindness he takes us firmly by the hand and leads us into a radical life-change.*
> — ROMANS 2:4 (MSG)

I wrote the words on a piece of paper and reread them several times over the next few days.

> *In kindness (in love)*
> *He leads us*
> *By the hand*
> *Into a radical life-change.*

One morning as I pondered those phrases, God gave me a vision of myself as a five-year-old boy with

Jesus. Jesus was firmly holding my hand, and we were walking to a new place that I did not recognize, and like a five-year-old, I was trying to pull away, but He wasn't letting go. He was leading me as a loving Father would do.

He was going to take me someplace I had never seen and could not understand until I experienced it with Him. I had to trust Jesus to know the way. He had a vantage point I did not, and He could see the destination.

Jesus was going to show me His love so I could love as He loves me. He would show me with a journey, not a destination.

IMPATIENCE

I learn best by hearing, so there were many days when I listened to God's Word and went into my prayer closet—an actual closet-size room in our home where I read Scripture and pray almost every morning—and then stepped into my day at work, confident that God had made His truth plain to me. Then the troubles of the world or challenges at work would distract me, and I would return to Him multiple times throughout the day, asking Him again to share His perspective: *Lord, help me to walk in the Spirit and to hear Your voice. Am I on track? What do You want me to do today? I have no idea how to solve this problem other than to depend on You and walk it out day by day.*

I would also get an idea for the company—one I was certain would work—and I would bring it to the office and start to implement it right away. People would drop other things they were working on because of my impatience, and my idea might end up hurting more than it helped because the wheels would come off some other project.

That's not how God worked with me. He didn't address all my issues at once, and I sometimes grew impatient with Him, despite His incredible blessings. God continued transforming me a little bit almost every day. Sometimes we didn't completely fix a particular issue before moving on to the next one—I'll be working on some issues for the rest of my life. I am not making excuses. I have just learned that sometimes the Lord peels me back like an onion. Sometimes it's one layer at a time, sometimes it's all the way through, and sometimes He peels a few layers back, we move on to something else, and then finish when He is ready.

Still, I wasn't satisfied with the pace of change. That was one of the problems God was working on, my impatience. I was ready to be done with my radical transformation. *Give me a list*, I prayed, *and I'll check them off*.

He said, again, "No, son. You keep asking that, but I reveal a little bit of your sin and your unholiness to you, and you turn from it. Then I can fill the space with more of My love. You're seeing why you shouldn't be living the way you are now, and when you do that, you say, 'God, take that out of me and replace it.' I don't want you to just check it off. I want you to understand it so you can be transformed by the renewing of your mind, which changes your heart, which changes how you live."

"Trust Me today," He said. "We'll do a little bit more every day. It's not going to be an easy process, and I'm going to reveal a lot to you about yourself."

Then God reminded me of a mentor of mine from years earlier who told me there are no shortcuts to transformation. Instead, you have two options. You can embrace what God is saying and then study it, learn, and grow in Him, changing the way you think and live. Or you can drag it out, keep resisting or arguing with God, and keep thinking the way you're thinking today. That decision will prolong, or even prevent, the process of your transformation.

There was no easy way. I had to embrace God's process for me, dive in headfirst, and work through it—to pray for help, to not be afraid or intimidated. He knows when it's time for me to rest. He also knows the time I need to work.

Sometimes God said to me, "We've got to go deep right now, and we've got to go hard into this process, and I'm going to guide you through it. I want you to really study the Word, and I want you to spend more time in prayer."

God wants me to continually come back to Him and study His Word and try to understand what He is saying to me. But some days I'm tired. I go into my prayer closet and open my Bible, and it feels like work instead of joy. Even the prayer feels like work. I just need to relax.

Every time I feel that way, I sense God saying to me, "It's okay, son. Just love Me, thank Me, and worship Me for who I am. And that's all we need to do today."

That moment allows me to relax and changes my whole perspective. I'm able to open up and allow His blessings to flow through me.

The psalmist said, "Taste and see that the LORD is good; blessed is the one who takes refuge in him" (Psalm 34:8).

I love that image of tasting the goodness of God. It's so satisfying when I'm weary. Just relax and taste God's goodness and allow it to wash away weariness and impatience. It is about Jesus's love and our relationship—less of me so I can have more of Him.

LEARNING TO LOVE AND RESPECT

I knew the gospel, I knew the Bible, and I had a relationship with Jesus. I was told what love was, but I didn't really know and understand and experience it with Him. My relationship with Jesus was in my head, not in my heart, and it was time for me to learn His love so I could love as He loves me.

The journey began with Tracy, although not always as God intended. I was so harsh with Tracy—until my mom called me out. I know it was God's grace that led to a front-porch conversation with my mother, who warned that if I didn't stop speaking harshly to Tracy, our marriage might not survive. I made a commitment to Tracy and to myself to change, and those few words from my mom changed the trajectory of my marriage.

That was early in our marriage, and with God's help, I learned to speak more respectfully and more lovingly. Ten years later, God began to show me that even though I was saying the right words, I was still not loving or respecting Tracy as I should.

I had grown up in a male-dominated family where wives cooked and cleaned and husbands were in charge. I thought I had moved on from that old way of thinking.

Tracy had been working in information technology at Cap Gemini Ernst & Young, a multinational IT and consulting company, and then at JCPenney. IT was populated mostly by men, and she was often the only woman in the room at work. That didn't slow her at all. Her responsibilities and leadership were growing at JCPenney as she was helping to develop IT strategy for a multibillion-dollar company.

Then at night she kept the books for our home-building company. That's where I saw her professional value—as a bookkeeper. We sometimes discussed how information technology could help us at the company—even considering the possibility of Tracy coming to work with us. Twice she attempted to resign, and both times JCPenney responded by giving her a raise. They valued IT and Tracy more than I did. I didn't like working in information technology and believed IT lived somewhere in the background—something you couldn't see that might help us improve around the edges.

Drawing and estimating and purchasing and hiring people who built houses with their hands—in my mind, those were the drivers of success in home-building. To me, people working in these areas created profit, and people in IT cost us profit. I looked forward to working with Tracy, but I didn't expect her contribution to be critical to our success. Looking back, I would say that I valued Tracy as my wife who did what I asked, and I valued the work she did as my employee. That is a difficult self-assessment to acknowledge, but I want you to understand my starting point.

Tracy resigned from JCPenney in 2011 to come work with us, and she didn't expect to find us so far behind in our information technology. The first week she started work, she saw our big whiteboard where we tracked all of our projects. Everything was up there—where the houses were on the ground and what stage they were in, what was next, and so on.

Tracy looked at the board and kind of turned pale. "What happens to a house when you're done?" she asked.

Well, we just wiped it off the board.

Out of respect for everyone in the room, Tracy hid the anxiety attack she felt coming on, and she calmly said, "Okay. Let's see if we can put systems in place to track these things."

We thought we were just fine.

She immediately set out to learn every process in the company because she knew information technology could have a positive impact on the management of every step. The company had gotten here by following God and working hard, so I was thinking, *Don't tell us that what we are doing is wrong or that our systems are wrong. We've grown on average 85 percent year over year since we started.* I was not yet on board with where she thought we should go. She was the new employee.

Yet Tracy was moving full speed, and I was wondering, *Why?*

Then Tracy and God shook me up. I mean they *really* shook me up.

Tracy saw how I respected the employees at work every day and how I took her for granted. She was my wife, after all. Anybody else might leave for another company.

"John," she said one day, "you love your staff and your employees way better than you love me."

That was like a punch in the gut. She had never said anything like that before. I tried to defend myself, but they were just words.

That night and the next morning, I prayed, asking God for some clarity, and He spoke to me the way my mother had when she pulled me aside on the front porch. "Son, she's right," He said. "You don't see your wife as I see her. She is my daughter, and I have given her gifts, and you need to recognize them and encourage her to be the woman of God I have called her and created her to be, preparing her to stand before Me and not holding her back. You have a wife who loves you, respects you, and is a gifted top-flight information technology professional ready and able to help you transform the company, and you can't even see it. I created opportunities for her to grow in her technical and leadership skills. I brought her to you, and you're ignoring all that. Not only that, you still don't love her the way I love her. It's time, son. It's time."

It broke my heart that I had not seen Tracy in that way. *Show me, God*, I prayed. *Please, please show me Tracy as You see her so I can value her and love her more like You do.*

Then God began to reveal Himself to me in my spirit, as He promised:

"What no eye has seen, What no ear has heard, and what no human mind has conceived"—the things God has prepared for those who love him—these are the things God has revealed to us by his Spirit. The Spirit searches all things, even the deep things of God

—1 CORINTHIANS 2:9–10

Deep in my heart, the Spirit revealed Tracy in ways that words cannot describe other than to say that I began to see her, her heart for Jesus and for me, and the gifts He had given her. He wasn't just teaching me; He was showing me. God led me to begin to speak life and encouragement over her, sharing what God was showing me about who she was in Him, gentle and respectful. He told me, "You have never valued her in this way, so give her time to begin to receive this new level of respect from you. It might take months or even years, but remain faithful and loving."

I confessed to Tracy and asked for her forgiveness, and I asked her to remind me to be gentle. Tracy was wise in her choice of words and her timing. In situations when I spoke too strongly, she didn't respond in the moment. She waited until we were both in a better place, and then she said, "Remember the other day when you said . . . ?" She didn't have to say another word. I remembered the time and my words, and the Holy Spirit corrected me.

In my time with God's Word, He gave me verses about gentleness that I could carry with me as a constant reminder:

Be completely humble and gentle; be patient, bearing with one another in love.

—EPHESIANS 4:2

Let your gentleness be evident to all. The Lord is near.

—PHILIPPIANS 4:5

Therefore, as God's chosen people, holy and dearly loved, clothe yourselves with compassion, kindness, humility, gentleness and patience.

—COLOSSIANS 3:12

I was not changed overnight—my love and respect for Tracy still grow. We have a counselor who helps us strengthen our marriage, and he told us we have the hardest type of marriage to maintain. "You work together, you do ministry together, you do family together—everything you do in your lives you do together. All of those things bring tension and stress to your marriage."

Thankfully, God gives us grace and wisdom.

At the office, for example, we learned quickly that we needed to avoid disagreements in meetings. Normally it's healthy to have discussions among senior leaders in meetings to work out issues where we might disagree. But when a husband and wife have those discussions in front of the staff, someone might think one of us is disrespecting the other. So if we anticipate disagreement, we talk through that ahead of time.

Tracy and I still butt heads occasionally, and she will ask me, "Are you going to let me do my job?" Other days I'll ask her the same question.

One of God's greatest gifts to me in this world was the day Tracy came to work with me day to day. I could write entire chapters about the ways she delivered on the promise of technology, enabling us to grow from fifty houses completed a year to more than five hundred. We could not have done that without her leadership and the tools she brought to the table.

More than that, working alongside her every day has made me a more loving husband and father and a more loving leader to the people who come to work at our company.

HEARTFELT
GENEROSITY

*O*ne of the biggest issues I've struggled with over the years was my assumption that if I gave to God financially, He would give back to me financially. There was a season when I said, *God, when's my payday? You know I've been busting my rear for You for years. Every time You asked me to do something, I did it to the best of my ability. You asked me to reach people for Christ, and that's what I tried to do. You asked me to give money, and I gave it. But God, I still have debt myself. I still have student loans, car payments, and a house payment. And You're telling us to give away all this money. When do I get mine?*

I didn't realize that my way of thinking was warped and not biblically sound. My thoughts were the opposite of generosity, the opposite of denying myself.

When I was younger, I saw John 15:5 as some sort of financial or tangible reward: "I am the vine; you are the branches. If you remain in me and I in you, you will bear much fruit; apart from me you can do nothing."

I took Luke 6:38 literally: "Give, and it will be given to you. Good measure, pressed down, shaken together, running over, will be put into your lap" (ESV).

Since the first day our company opened, the world would have said we were generous. I was quick to tell people, "This is God's company, not mine." We tithed corporate profits, and we were doing our best to fulfill the mission God had given us.

I knew the principles of generosity, and I was following them. I felt we were doing everything by the book. But by the heart? Maybe not. I didn't fully understand why God wanted us to be generous or how it really helped.

Unfortunately—and it hurts me to even say this—I was giving more out of obedience but also with an expectation that I would get more. I was overemphasizing and misunderstanding Luke 6:38, believing that the more money we made and the more successful we became in the world's eyes, the more I deserved something and felt like it was mine. That's the opposite of God's heart. First Corinthians 13:3 says, "If I give away all I have, and if I deliver up my body to be burned, but have not love, I gain nothing" (ESV).

I could tithe and I could give because God told me to, but without love it was for nothing. If He transformed my heart, then I would give because I *wanted* to—because of His great love for me and because He was first generous to me, and I love Him and want others to know that love.

Jesus watched a poor widow who gave two small coins, all she had, to the temple treasury, and said that this woman had given more than all of the rich, who were giving only a portion of their wealth. Reading that story, I prayed, *God, help me to know Your love more so I can love more like You. I know Psalm 24:1 says, "The earth is the LORD's, and everything in it." The world and all its people belong to You. So, Jesus, please change my way of thinking to truly know and believe in my mind and heart that it is all Yours—my life, Tracy, our kids, the business, and every dollar. Help me to die to myself and give out of love as the poor widow gave.*

I prayed for a heart like the poor widow's, then God began to show me why He wants us to be generous. He said, "Because I am generous, I gave up My life for yours while you were still a sinner so you could have everlasting life. I want more people to know this love. You give in My name from a loving heart so that others know Me and My great love for them."

When I began to see generosity as less about money and more about Him and His great love, then I became much more generous. My giving had been transactional, but it became relational out of His great love and His desire for others to experience that with Him.

THE OWNER PUTS
ME ON SALARY
AND FREES ME

*E*very year I would take time away for prayer and to ask God how much He wanted us to give that year. We would be working on our budget for the company, deciding how much to invest in property, how many homes we would build. Our goals for reaching people for Christ and giving to the kingdom were all a part of that conversation.

Then God told me my perspective was backward.

"Son," He said, "it is time to get off the milk and on to the meat."

I thought, *Uh oh, this is going to be a tough conversation.*

He went on to say, "Everywhere you go, you're telling people, 'This is God's business, not my business.' You say you don't own the business but that I do. Really? When you were working for other people, did you ever ask them how much of their money you could give away? Of course not. It was their business and their money. You had no right to ask that. So if this is My company, then why are you asking Me how much of My money you should give away? If this is My company, then it's all My money, and you should be asking how much I want to pay you to do My work."

I had to spend some time with that. If this is truly God's company, and I'm working for Him simply stewarding His company, then all of it, including the profits, belong to Him, not me.

God was putting me on salary.

For the first five years we were in business, I didn't get paid. Once I did, my income was based on the company profits, after expenses, our tithe and gifts, and reinvestments in the company. That's typically the way the owners of small companies operate.

Tracy and I talked and prayed about what the Lord was saying and agreed that it was time for me to go on salary. We did some research and determined what the fair market value for my work was, and we put me on a salary for that amount (which was about 30 percent less than what I had been taking), just like everybody else working for the company. The rest belonged to God, and it was either reinvested in the company or given to the kingdom, whichever the Lord (the owner) wanted.

I look back on that decision and thank God that He did that for me, because He used that discipline to protect my heart and my family's heart. We don't see extra money in the company and wonder, "Wouldn't it be nice if we could . . . ?" We budget to our income and live within our means.

Even now, as an employee of God's company, before we make a major purchase, I consult with Tracy, Chad (our CFO), and one of my Spirit-led counselors and ask them to pray with me to see if God is okay with us spending this money. I don't have exclusive access to God's wisdom. Sometimes the Lord says yes, other times He says now is not the right time.

I still need to humble myself before God and man and allow others to help me make wise choices when it comes to money and other things. And I continue to ask the Lord to search my heart and show me the temptation that comes from my own desires, as in James 1:14–15, so I can turn from it before it gives birth to sinful actions. God shows me my evil desires, and I ask Him to teach me His way and help my heart to go after Him. He does.

I don't believe greed is still rooted in my heart, but it may always be a thorn in my flesh. Remnants of greed, anger, and other sins remain. Those are real thorns that I have to deal with, and God might never take those completely away from me in this life. In fact, He may leave those things there on purpose so that I become more dependent on Him, having to die to myself more and more each day.

The challenge never seems to fully go away. But understanding that God only wants what is best for me has been a freeing experience.

I try to model God's heart of infinite generosity, but in all honesty, I don't think I will arrive until I stand before the Lord. Without His perspective, I want what I believe is rightfully mine. But if I continually ask Christ to reveal what He wants for me and ask Him to transform my way of thinking and my heart, it will completely change the way I live as a man of God, a husband, a father, and a leader.

NEW
RELATIONSHIPS,
NEW
OPPORTUNITIES

When we build a home for a customer, we work closely with them for six to nine months, depending on the size of the house. Over the months, more than a few people from our team become friends with them—sometimes close friends—as we try to model the love of Christ. This is such an exciting and sometimes stressful time in our customers' lives as they transition to their new home. We guide them through the process, encouraging them, supporting them, and often praying with them.

Then they close on the house, we hand them the keys, and all of a sudden, it's over.

In the neighborhoods we develop, we keep model homes open, and our sales staff is there every day maintaining relationships, but we wanted more. We wanted a way to maintain a closer relationship with the friends we make through the building process. We tried several things over time to maintain that inter-action. We haven't mastered it, but we're getting better.

One simple thing we do is ask folks in our customer relationship department to be sensitive to opportunities that might come up when they're on the phone. Like when a customer said she was going to have surgery in a couple of days, and the customer service rep asked her supervisor if we could send the customer flowers. Of course, we could, and we did.

For years we used one title company to handle all of our real estate closings, and that company was closely affiliated with a bank where we did most of our business. We grew to become one of the title company's largest customers, with hundreds of closings every year, and each transaction gave us a touch point to share the love of Jesus with everybody sitting around the closing table. The staff and the president of the company took great care of us through the years.

As our company grew, and we sold more homes, I began to sense God telling me that we were missing opportunities to do more of His work through our closings. If we could partner with the title company or handle that work ourselves, we could continue the interaction to reach people for Christ and give more tithe to God's kingdom.

Of course, if we started our own title company, the company we had been working with for years would lose all that business overnight, and a lot of their employees would be affected. Some would lose their jobs. We didn't want that to happen. I asked our executive team and my pastor to pray about it. Even some pastors from other churches were praying with us. Before I approached the title company's president with the possibility of a partnership, I wanted to confirm that it was God's will and not greed or selfishness. After weeks of prayer, we all believed God was saying this was the direction to take.

I went to the president of the company to talk about our options. My first preference, I said, was to partner with his company. I explained that we would want to tithe 20 percent of the profits to God's kingdom and that I was certain our growth together would more than offset the giving. In the end, I believed his share of the profits would be even more.

He disagreed and pretty much cut off the conversation. They couldn't give that much money and stay in business. So we left things as they were, and I continued to pray for guidance.

Then God gave me a solution that I thought would allow the title company to continue to grow its profits with us. I went back to the president and explained that we would leave all of our business with his company, every closing plus the growth we anticipated, but we would ask him to tithe 20 percent of the profits from our closings—just our closings. We would ask him to put that money into a fund that we could manage together, with half going to his church and half going to ours.

"The only reason I want to do this," I said, "is to further the kingdom."

That too was not an option for him.

This issue continued to weigh on me. I truly believed God wanted us to give a portion of the profits from our closings to do His work, but He also wanted us to do it in a way that not only preserved our relationship with the title company but also enhanced it. I felt God telling me to spend more time with the president, so I went to him and asked for that opportunity. He was a Christian and active in his church, and I suggested, "I'd like to meet with you once a month to pray together, grow in Christ, and share what the Lord is doing in each other's hearts and lives. I think the Lord wants us to grow together in Him." (This wasn't someone I had just met—he and I had many conversations about the Lord and our faith for more than ten years.)

He said he didn't want to do that, and I was running out of options.

After a few days in prayer, I went back to him and said, "I'd like to follow biblical principles here. Let's meet again. You bring your pastor and I'll bring my pastor, the way the Bible lays it out. We can all pray together, talk through the issues, and pray together and see what the Lord wants. That's all we want."

The answer again was no.

I said I was sorry, but I didn't see any option other than to create our own title company.

Please understand that this is my perspective and may not be the president's. There are times in business when two Christians disagree about how to handle a certain situation. My job is not to question whether the other person is hearing God but rather to do what I believe God is calling me to do. The bottom line in this situation was that he was being faithful and obedient to what he felt the Lord was telling him to do as His steward. So I am not saying any of this to be negative toward him. I believe he was following the Lord and I believe I was, and we both had to be faithful, even if it didn't play out the way I wanted at the time.

In addition to our closing business, we had a $6 million line of credit with the bank it was affiliated with. Soon after that final meeting, we received written notice that we had sixty days to pay off the line. I went straight to Chad Miles, our chief financial officer, and we both knew the immediate demand for all that cash to pay off the line could put us out of business. We assumed the bank knew that, and this was their effort to force us to change course on the title company in order to protect their business, their staff, and their shareholders.

I left Chad's office, and we both felt the Lord was assuring us that He was with us. But we couldn't imagine how He might pull us through. I continued to pray, *Jesus, we believe this is Your plan and we have sought Spirit-led wise counsel. If this is Your will, then help us figure out how to solve this problem. If it is not, let us know so we do not start this title company. Just let Your will be done. You're going to have to show up now with a solution.*

I honestly believed this was God's problem, not ours, and I continued to feel His peace. I believed His solution, whatever it was, would save the company. But my flesh was weak, so sometimes I would wonder and have to pray and give it to God all over again.

Over the next two months, we saw a pattern we had seen years earlier when God had asked Tracy and me to give Him all of our cash. A surprisingly large number of people decided to close early on their homes. Other companies that owed us money accelerated their payments. Then our tax accountant called Chad and said they found a tax credit that we had not been taking. We had been putting too much money into the escrow account every month to pay our taxes at the end of the fiscal year—more than $2 million. That was cash out of the blue.

And then there was this: We had been developing our Bryson subdivision and were preparing to close the loan with the bank. As it turned out, however, the person in our company responsible for managing the finances on that development had neglected to take the draws from our line of credit at the bank for months. We had been developing the subdivision with cash flow instead of borrowed money. So when we closed on the sale of the lots to homebuilders, they wrote their checks to us, and we didn't owe anything to the bank. That gave us an unexpected $600,000. I am convinced that God allowed that $600,000 "mistake" to happen as a reminder to us that He is in control.

All those things came together, and less than sixty days after we received the notice, we were able to write a $6 million check to the bank. Only God can orchestrate all those things coming together and in perfect timing.

The result still was not what we had hoped for. We wanted to keep our business at the bank, and most importantly we wanted to keep the relationship with the president and his team. But when God planted an idea to go a different direction, He showed up in exciting ways we had not anticipated, opening doors to new personal connections and opportunities to give more to His kingdom. I believe He did this for us and for the president of the title company/bank, whom I still consider a friend. We are both accountable to the Lord, and He is faithful and just.

STEADFAST
HOMES

*I*n 2014, I believed rising home prices were opening another opportunity for us to reach a different people group for Christ. One of the largest national homebuilding companies introduced a line of smaller, lower-priced homes for buyers on a tighter budget. We had been in business for nearly a decade at that point, and our company was still growing. The national homebuilder had a good idea for reaching a market they had been missing, and it didn't take me long to figure out how we could reach that market too. We had started and expanded a successful homebuilding company, so we could do that again.

It's an experience that I remind myself of frequently, because God didn't tell me to start Steadfast Homes. I thought I was smart enough to start it on my own. I applied the same principles we were using for our principal company, and I knew a lot more than I had when I started out nearly a decade earlier.

Building high-quality smaller homes could actually be simpler, like building an apartment on a slab. Homebuilding is homebuilding, right?

The difference was I hadn't asked God if I should do it. I just came up with a great idea of starting a lower price point homebuilding company and then did it.

But it didn't work. Nothing about the concept worked for us, and we had to shut the company down a couple of years later after it had cost us about half a million dollars.

I learned so many lessons from that experience. First, I am constantly reminded that the businesses we operate are blessed because they are God's, and He is in them. We constantly ask for His guidance. The time when I decided to do it on my own, I took control of the decisions and the outcomes. Without realizing it, I had decided I didn't need God for that one, because I already knew everything I needed to know. I thought I was smarter than I really was, and in the process, I took away the blessing of God's hand being on us.

Now when I have an idea, I try to ask the Lord three questions: *Lord, are You asking me to do this? Are You asking us to partner with someone to do this? Or are You asking us to pass this idea on to someone else to do it?*

Of course, I know unbelievers who have great homebuilding companies. I don't know how they built those companies, but for me as a Christ follower and as a son of God, my relationship is with God, and He is constantly trying to keep me dependent on Him to do His will. He allows me to go and do what I want to do, even if I don't ask Him first, but that doesn't mean He's going to bless it or allow it to succeed.

The roots of my understanding go back to the old person that I was. Years before we started the home-building company, God allowed me to be successful without Him for a while. Then we were forced to file for bankruptcy. We lost everything we had.

The Steadfast Homes experience reminded me again that I should abide in the Lord, depending on Him for everything. He has allowed me to get to where we are today, and He is just asking me to love Him, love people, make disciples, and bring glory to Him.

Here's another lesson I learned through Steadfast Homes: If something isn't working, and you realize God is not in it, shut it down. It's human nature, whenever you have acted on a great idea, to take pride in it and bring it to God and expect Him to bless it. But God is not interested in blessing what I or other people think is great. You never see that illustrated in Scripture. He blesses *His* ideas, His will for His glory.

Yet we go forward with our own idea, investing people, time, and money. My experience has been that without God's blessing, the idea fails. Then what?

You can keep trying to lean into it, but that's just running in the wrong direction. I've learned the hard way that I just have to stop, ask God for directions, and turn myself around.

With Steadfast Homes, the longer we kept running, the more money we lost, the more time we wasted, and the more people who got hurt. So we shut it down.

I remind myself so I don't make the same dumb mistake again.

During those times where things don't work out the way we thought, it doesn't mean the Shepherd didn't show up. He never left me. I left His plan and turned away from His will in that area. There are a lot of other factors that go into it, and we just have to continue to hear His voice and say, *God, I may not fully understand, but I'm going to trust You through the process and get back in Your will.*

FEAR

*T*he housing market had emerged from the recession, and we were doing well with our development company as well as with a mortgage company and a home warranty company we had started. We had also increased our offering to the church to support a building program.

About three months earlier, I was reading the Genesis story of Joseph interpreting Pharaoh's dream. Joseph predicted seven years of good years followed by seven years of famine, and he advised Pharaoh to store up for the famine.

I felt the Lord speaking to me through the story, but I wasn't sure what He was saying. I spent a week or two asking Him to clarify and concluded that God wanted us to store up for a coming famine. I felt the Lord was saying, "*Save* and prepare." I decided to cut back on our offering (not our tithe) and save those extra funds.

At the office the next day, I told Chad to make the change. I hadn't told Tracy or anyone else about the decision—not even our executive team or our pastor. We were still tithing, and I felt confident that the Lord was leading me in this decision. Then we experienced a slight decrease in our sales and profits despite the fact that the overall market was doing great. I saw our downturn as a sign of another possible recession on the horizon. Business in our market was booming, in part because the overall Dallas–Fort Worth market had done so well since the end of the recession. Buyers were pouring into our area. I mean, it was almost impossible to build the wrong house, because people were buying anything. Yet our sales and profits had hit a big bump in the road.

I asked our pastor, Scott Wilson, if Tracy and I could come to his office to pray together, hoping the Lord might help us understand what was coming. In addition to being our pastor, Scott is one of my dearest friends. He and his wife, Jenni, live across the road from us, and I often ask him to pray with me when I'm seeking clarity. We had been friends before I started building houses. We had grown up together as adults. I told him what we were experiencing with our business, and the three of us prayed for understanding. This was just the opposite of everything we had experienced for the life of the company.

As we prayed, Scott said, "I keep feeling I should ask you if anything has changed regarding your giving."

"No," Tracy said.

I knew exactly what Scott was talking about, even though he didn't, and I said, "Well, yeah, I made a shift."

Scott said, "Oh," and Tracy looked at me like, *What?*

I told them that I had cut our giving in half in anticipation of difficult financial times ahead.

I instantly recognized my mistake. I had isolated myself in my decision to cut our giving, and Satan had used my own mind and my fear of a recession—fear that I hadn't even recognized myself—to tell me I'd better start putting extra money away. In my logic, that made sense. I could line it up with the Word, and I never sought any wise counsel from others before making my decision. Just before I talked to Chad, I remember thinking, *I don't really need their input. This is my decision, and I'm going to do this.*

In reality, Satan wanted me to cut back on our giving because God will withhold His blessings unless we're being good stewards with what He gives us. I wasn't stewarding God's resources the way He wanted me to. The Lord had asked us to give tithe and offering to grow our faith in Him. Satan wanted me to reduce our gifts, and he used the fear in my own heart as the stepping stone to get me to do it.

The Lord taught me, though, that I should have sought the wise counsel of other Christians before making my decision. He revealed to me that the attitude of my heart (believing I didn't need advice on this decision) allowed Satan to have his way. Then Tracy and I prayed together to seek God's will, and He reminded me of all the times He has shown Himself faithful. He showed me He was telling me there was a famine coming and to store up. But what He meant was to increase our giving, storing even more up in heavenly barns, for there your barns will be filled to overflowing. However, the fear in my own heart did not allow me to even consider that as part of what the Lord was speaking.

We did increase our tithe and offering, and sales and profits increased. It doesn't mean we won't go through a famine, but it does mean that I know, understand, and trust the Lord a little more after going through this. I will follow Him, seeking His wisdom through my prayers and His Scripture as well as the Spirit-led counsel of others, and God will take care of the outcome.

MULTIPLYING
THE POWER OF
GOD'S VOICE

*O*ne day a team leader asked if I could share with him the process I use for hearing from the Lord. I told him I couldn't do that as CEO, but as a brother in Christ I would be happy to. Whether you own the company or work for someone else, you can share the gospel and teach people to pray. But how we present it matters—not as the boss but as a person who can share the hope that is within you.

Twenty years earlier in chapel as a student at Southwestern Assemblies of God University, I had learned to begin my day in prayer and Scripture. My prayers, I learned, should be spent mostly listening and writing down everything I thought the Lord was saying to me. Then I would go to the Bible, and the words I had written that aligned with Scripture were God's words for me.*

Our team leader and I met, I explained all of this, and we scheduled times to pray together. Less than a week later, another leader asked if I could help him learn to hear God's voice, and then a few days later another asked.

---

* To learn more about my process, go to https://meetjohnhouston.com/resources to get a PDF download and journal prompts for you to use.

I try to see patterns in my life and seek meaning in them. This was clearly one of those, so I prayed, *Okay, God, what are You doing here?*

I felt Him saying, "I'm stirring the hearts of your leaders so they want to know Me in a new way."

So instead of scheduling individual times with the three leaders, I invited all of our top-level leaders to meet once a month for a year at my house. We talked through the process my professor had taught me and grew into it.

For the first ten or fifteen minutes of each meeting, I shared Scripture with them about prayer and about hearing from God, and I shared details of how God was speaking to me. It was important that I not do all the talking—we all had different experiences that might help others understand.

Then for fifteen or twenty minutes, we prayed individually, listened, and wrote what God was saying to us. They didn't all do it just as I did, because God speaks to each of us differently. But the same God was speaking to all of us.

Then something more powerful happened. As more of our top leaders began to hear God's voice more clearly, they brought God's wisdom and creativity into our decision-making.

God began to transform our company's leadership through those prayers and then to transform our company. He gave them words that lined up with what He was telling others when it came to decisions we were facing, and we then knew He was giving us clear direction.

I was reminded of a time years earlier when Tracy was working for Cap Gemini Ernst & Young. They had a major IT problem that was costing the company millions of dollars. They had all these leading engineers, some of the best in the business, working on the code, and nobody could figure it out. Tracy was working with them but wasn't having any more success than anybody else. Then she went to the bathroom and prayed, *God, You've got to show up, because we've got to solve this problem*. Then she waited. And as she waited quietly there in the bathroom, the code came to her. Literally, she had the answer. God had given her the code. She went to the lead engineer and said, "Try this," and it worked.

The lesson for me from Tracy's experience, which I have shared many times, is if you have a relationship with Jesus, His Holy Spirit is in you, and He wants to guide you in every circumstance. That's the vision I

want every person working in our family of companies to catch, so that when God speaks to them and
through them, they're confident and willing to step
up and say, "I believe the Lord is telling me to do
that, to seek the Word of God and wise counsel for
confirmation."

It's up to me to do more than just pray, *God, please
send somebody.*

Maybe I am that somebody.

Don't just pray, *God, please fix this.*

Instead, pray, *God, what is my part in fixing this?
Jesus, through Your Holy Spirit give me Your thoughts,
ideas, and creativity to solve this.* Then listen and share
what the Lord is putting on your mind. If it lines up
with the Word of God, trust Him and follow Him.

TRANSFORMING PROJECT TRANSFORMS A COMMUNITY

*T*hrough our company, we were creating short-term mission opportunities, often internationally. Then our staff began seeking opportunities to make an impact on the people around us, our nearest neighbors. They were right, of course, and we didn't have to look far to find those opportunities.

A single mother in Waxahachie had breast cancer, and the home she and her children were living in had serious issues that needed to be addressed. Along with our subcontractors and suppliers, we had the skills to make the repairs she needed. One of our superintendents spent a week at her house getting the place ready so we could bring in teams and get the work done in a couple of days. By then we had volunteers from our office staff as well as subcontractors and suppliers. Friday morning came, and everybody had their assignments. We worked two shifts on Friday and again on Saturday transforming that house and opening our eyes to even more possibilities close by.

The mayor of Waxahachie told me about a shelter for women and children that needed help updating the living areas. We spent some time at the shelter (which was a big, rambling house) assessing the problems and realized this was going to be a big project.

The operator of the shelter was renting the house, and we wanted to be good stewards of what God had given us. We got a commitment from the owner that if we invested in this house and made these improvements, he would continue to allow the shelter to operate there without raising the rent for a certain period of time. We made a commitment together, and years later the home still offers shelter to women and children.

We took on more projects refurbishing homes, one in the spring and one in the fall for a couple of years, and we began to understand that God might be creating opportunities for something even bigger. As it turned out, we weren't the only ones in the community thinking along those lines.

Andy Lehman, local and global missions pastor at The Oaks Church, and Casey Ballard, executive director of the United Way, founded the Waxahachie Project to assess community needs and help coordinate organizations and individuals who wanted to offer help. Andy and Casey organized a meeting of more than sixty community leaders from churches, civic groups, businesses, and the government to discuss how we could work together with our strengths to address needs in the community.

Soon the project leadership developed a mission statement:

> *The Waxahachie Project's vision is to unite community leaders, business leaders, non-profits, churches, and educational institutions to work for the good of our city. We do that by embracing a shared understanding of Waxahachie's greatest needs and strengths and measures for continual health and growth. Our heart is to serve and celebrate the many people and organizations already doing so much good for our city. We do that by providing a vehicle by which leaders can work together toward common goals that will make our great city of Waxahachie an even greater place to work and live.*

The first step for the project was to identify the needs and the resources, as defined by the community itself. We reached out to OneHope and Rob Hoskins, who had been essential to the development of Tracy's and my stewardship strategy to help. OneHope created a survey that more than three hundred students from Southwestern Assemblies of God University took door-to-door throughout the city. The survey sought answers to three key questions:

1. What are we doing well that we can maximize—together?
2. What do we need the most help in—that we can address together?
3. Where are the gaps between services and needs—how can we close them together?

Among the greatest strengths identified was our sense of community and the collaboration among civic organizations and churches to tackle issues. Among the greatest needs were building affordable housing, creating more employment opportunities, and healing the racial divide experienced by so many communities.

The mayor told us about an African American church in town that was in dire need of assistance. Taking on a project like that could create new relationships between people and communities who had not worked together. This was a very special congregation. In 1864, a group of slaves had come together to worship Christ under an oak tree in east Waxahachie. Later that year they formed the Samaria Missionary

Baptist Church, purchased a lot across the street from the oak tree, and began construction of their first church. Almost immediately the church became a stop on the Underground Railroad as runaway slaves hid there during the daytime.

Over the next 150-plus years, the church was remodeled multiple times and rebuilt after a fire in 1915. But by 2016, the building was deteriorating badly, and the congregation didn't have the financial resources to address the problems.

The opportunity, the mayor told us, was bigger than repairing a historic church. We could help repair our community, working alongside each other in the name of Christ.

If all we had wanted to do was help fix a church, we could have written a check to fund the project. We have the expertise to hire painters and subcontractors to take care of the whole thing. But we wanted to reach people and let them know we love them. And we wanted volunteers to have an opportunity to be a part of something bigger—to be a part of the kingdom and experience Jesus in this way.

More than 250 volunteers from all over Ellis County gave their time or donated supplies and materials.

Other businesspeople, churches, and pastors participated, and the relationships that grew from that experience are still building bridges among congregations and individuals.

God had something way broader in mind for us when our pastor, Scott Wilson, connected us with John Maxwell, one of the most powerful, positive leadership communicators in the world. Scott had met John at an event where John was speaking, and they stayed in touch.

John had trained millions of leaders through seminars, best-selling books, tapes, and other training tools. Then traveling internationally, he met good people in leadership who were unable to reach their potential because they lacked the training necessary to equip them. The world needed the gifts God had given to John.

That's when John and his team created the EQUIP program and trained more than 5 million leaders outside the United States in just the first few years. In 2013, he took 150 coaches who had been through his training program to Guatemala, where in a week they trained nearly 24,000 people who would then train 350,000 others in values-based leadership.

John invited Scott to go to Guatemala with him to see the transformation firsthand, and Scott asked me and a couple of other guys from church to join him.

In Central America, I saw John Maxwell's heart for coming alongside people and adding value with the influence God gave him. John had begun his career as a pastor, and he made a huge impact on saved people. Then he believed God was calling him into the world to speak to people, with a secular message based on God's Word. He didn't make his message preachy, just powerful. The more time I spent with him, the more I saw his heart for reaching people.

John believes that when 10 percent of the people in a community or country engage in the transformative process grounded in positive values, they reach a tipping point that creates significant change. We witnessed that change occurring in communities in Guatemala.

Scott and I and the others from home believed John's program could add tremendously to the Waxahachie Project. He told us that he had not offered EQUIP in the United States, but he and his team would visit and see if there might be a fit.

He came and saw what we were already doing, and soon more than six thousand community leaders had participated in roundtable discussions and leadership programs presented by the John Maxwell Leadership Foundation. We had expanded to encompass all of Ellis County.

In 2018, John presented at the WX Leaders Summit, where he presented his Beyond Success seminar to hundreds of leaders. At the end of the day, after taking a short break, John invited anyone interested to remain to hear about his most important relationship and the source of his secrets of leadership. He was clear that he would be sharing his faith, and he wasn't pressuring anyone to stay. But those who did stay heard an eloquent presentation of the gospel. More than fifty people responded to his invitation to know Christ, including a few of our own employees.

John has continued to invest in our community's transformation, personally presenting his values-based leadership lessons to hundreds of our leaders every year. His team from the John Maxwell Leadership Foundation shares principles in a roundtable setting that participants take back to their workplaces and families as they live out their leadership values.

Sometimes I meet people who are familiar with us, and they might say, "It's so great how your employees volunteer so much of their time in the community." Or somebody else says, "I'm excited about the Leadership Summit you're supporting."

Those people are seeing the subsets of our true purpose for the kingdom, and I'm okay with that.

I'm beginning to understand that staying focused on our purpose sometimes isn't so simple. We try to make sure that every opportunity to serve the community also serves our purpose. And we trust that God will guide us from His vantage point to the places He wants us to go—even when we can barely see the next step.

TRUST OPENS DOORS TO OUR LARGEST DEVELOPMENT

*T*he relationships God built through the Waxahachie Project impacted our community as a whole and many businesses individually. Then God used those relationships to help us with our company's own "Waxahachie project."

I came across eighty acres of land in Waxahachie just off Highway 77, and the property looked like something we might be interested in developing for single-family homes. A closer look, though, told me it might not work for us. Another piece of undeveloped property sat between this dirt and the closest water main and sewer line.

We called the owner of that other property and talked with him about the possibility of running water and sewer to the eighty acres I was looking at. He said we would have to work things out with the city and remarked, "Good luck with that."

He said he had a difficult relationship with city leaders—he didn't like them, and they didn't like him.

I spent some time with the maps before going any further and realized there was another three-hundred-acre undeveloped tract and another eighty-acre piece. Would it be possible to bring all that property together in a single deal? We didn't have cash for an investment nearly that big. A five-hundred-acre tract would take years to build out and require deep pockets. Our pockets were not that deep to pull all that off. And then there were the issues with the Waxahachie planning department.

I began to meet with the owners of the property and suggested that we work together with the city to come up with a master plan and that our development company develop it with them. They could put up the land as their investment, then we would do all of the development work. When we sold the lots, we would pay them for the property and give a percentage of the profit. That allowed us to develop without having to put up a lot of money for the dirt, and they were happy to let us work with the city.

God was in this whole project, but there is another cool step we saw God take. We had the property under contract and went to the city and told them what we were thinking, and it was like God gave us favor with everybody in the building. In fact, the city manager asked, "Do you mind if we are part of planning the master plan? We would be happy to pay the company of your choice to design the plan."

"Sounds great," I said. That was an absolute gift because the city was fully invested in the project. We all had the same goal in mind—to create a high-quality community—and the Waxahachie city leaders understood the positive impact of a couple thousand homes/apartments. Sharing and coordinating from the beginning would ensure we were on the same page for the entire project.

We brought in a planner and, at the city's suggestion, scheduled a three-day brainstorm and planning session. With all the right people in the room, we were able to develop a plan that was ready to go to the city council for approval in days, not months or years.

We worked together to streamline decisions, like when the school district told the city they thought they would need a school within a community that large. We had already designated a site, so we gave the property to the school district. The plan had a $9.2 million four-lane divided boulevard through the center of the development and worked with the city to create a public improvement district (PID) to pay for it. A PID is a short-term tax on homeowners in the development to pay for portions of the infrastructure. However, the city wanted the road built sooner than we were ready. I explained that we could pay about $6 million, but they would have to cover the balance. They came back quickly with a yes, and we were able to build one of the nicest roads in Waxahachie.

We never planned to buy five hundred acres for a single development in a housing recession. The only way I can explain it is that God had a plan for us and that property. God opened doors for us that we never expected. The most amazing part of this experience is hearing about all the people in that master plan subdivision who are being loved on, cared for, and have come to know Jesus because of relationships with other homeowners, the Bible studies that are happening in those homes, and the community engagement that is happening in this neighborhood as those homeowners reach people for Christ right where they live—loving their neighbors.

Through the Waxahachie Project and this project, I was reminded that many times we in the Christian world tend to get things backward. We pray to God for help, or we ask someone if they can do a favor for us instead of asking them what we can do for them, serving them and their needs. In this case, we worked with Waxahachie leadership for years, doing as much as we could to serve them because that is what we should do as men and women of Jesus, and then suddenly God brought this other opportunity that was so much bigger than us but all for His glory. Through the trusting relationships God had built, we were ready to develop a residential project that was bigger than anything we had ever considered, and I am the one blessed to play a part in the story God is writing in the lives of each person who lives in that subdivision and that city.

GOD DOES MORE
HEADHUNTING

When Terry Weaver was ready to retire from running our development company, we had grown so much we needed a highly skilled talent to run it. Danielle Depot, our vice president of sales and construction, suggested we reach out to Chip Boyd. He was running development for a large publicly traded homebuilding company where he had previously worked.

It is a long shot, I thought. Chip was known as one of the best developers in the business, and by that I mean in all of Dallas–Fort Worth. He wouldn't leave a big national company to join a small company like ours. But I felt God urging me to reach out, so Danielle called him to make the connection, and he agreed to talk.

Chip's career in the industry had been with public companies, where decisions every day all point to the quarterly Wall Street analysis. It's all about the quarterly projections and the annual bottom line for publicly traded companies.

"For lack of a better term," he told me, "it was a meat grinder. A high-stress, pressure-cooker environment that was focused less on people than on the numbers."

The bulk of Chip's work in the metroplex had been north, around McKinney, Allen, and Frisco. He didn't do any work down in Ellis County, so he didn't really know about our company.

The first thing he did was go to our website, where he watched a video of me describing how God told me one day that it was time to start a homebuilding company. "As a faith-based Christian," he says, "that hit me as something that was not only unusual but extremely endearing and powerful. So many times in the business world, my wife and I had been exposed to people who claim that on some level, but they don't necessarily live it. My initial thought was that it sounded good, but I was skeptical."

It's a small world, and an even smaller community of builders and developers, and if you treat people badly, they don't forget. So, it was easy for Chip to check our reputation with people he trusted. He met members of our executive team and began to understand that our mission statement is much more than a statement. When we talk about reaching people for Christ and giving to the kingdom, it's who we are, not just what we do. It's why we exist as a company.

Then we talked and prayed. He had legitimate concerns about moving from a huge company to a very small company. Our footprint had grown so fast; what if one of the giants came in and wanted to buy us out and immediately grab that market share? We made assurances regarding that and his other concerns, and Chip joined us.

"It became readily clear to me that this in fact was a leap of faith I needed to take," Chip says. "It's refreshing to come in and do work that's focused on something greater than the dollar. That doesn't mean we can't pursue the dollar. We have to. And it doesn't mean we aren't striving to be the greatest, most profitable businesses we can be. We are. But when you're doing it and feeling like you're led by God to be pursuing this mission, it makes all of the stresses that are typical in pursuit of those things far easier to absorb. And so that's been the greatest change."

Chip's experience and wisdom were vital to the success of our development company. Because our cycle times were so long in property development, there was a constant need to "feed the machine," as he described it. We were acquiring property that would not have homes for several years. So we were anticipating population growth patterns and real estate price trends with every decision.

It takes five good deals to make up for one bad one, so it was important to be diligent and prudent in what we went after from an acquisition standpoint. Chip gave us the experience and insight to make those decisions, but the best part was that I got to run this race with Chip. You see, Chip is great at development, but he is far better at pouring into and developing people to reach people for Christ and give to the kingdom while delivering excellence. He has taught me so much, and I am humbled to serve alongside him.

BETTER BEFORE
BIGGER

When the Lord told me to start the homebuilding company, I felt like He was telling me it would be a large production business. I didn't have any idea how many homes we would ultimately be building.

I was thinking that if we closed on thirty houses in a year, that would be a good start. As we got closer to thirty, I felt God saying our next goal should be 150. We got closer to 150, and He said our next goal should be 300.

We weren't ready to run a large company in the beginning. As the business grew, God gave us the wisdom and the resources to grow with it. God builds my faith, my trust, and my understanding of Him day by day. He has prepared me to take on much more today than I was able to twenty years ago, but I still have a lot to learn.

We came out of the recession stronger than ever. Everything God had given us had prospered, and I wondered what was coming next. In the midst of transforming my heart, God told me through my prayers that He wanted to transform our company.

For three months, I spent hours and hours praying and writing as I sought to understand what God desired of us. He made it clear to me that He wanted the company to grow to three or four times our current production, multiplying our opportunities to achieve God's purpose.

Before He could grow the company, and before we could maintain that growth, we would have to improve all of our systems and all of our processes, from invoicing to payroll to ordering to relationships with subcontractors and suppliers. We had to change almost everything, from our training to our website. Everything had to change before He could take us to the new place He had in mind for us.

And before we could transform our strategies and systems, we had to transform our hearts. Terry Trayvick, who has been developing our strategy for years, reminds us often, "If you don't have the right culture, it will eat your strategy alive. You'll never get to where you want to be without the right culture."

Our culture begins in our hearts—my heart and the heart of every person who works for our company. We had to do a better job of preparing our staff, creating the right experience for them from the time they begin the interview process all the way through the time they retire, walking through life with them and pouring our love into them—teaching, training, and preparing them to create a legacy for their lives and for their families for generations.

How do we live and lead with love, justice, and righteousness in every area of our life and represent Christ in those areas? We believe if you keep God first and keep your family second, then the business will take care of itself. We needed to get better at that before we could grow bigger.

We also had to get better at communicating our love. Sometimes we spoke in a language that only Christians understood, and some people were left to wonder what we were talking about. Several members of our team helped me learn to express love to all people.

We found out that if someone had not accepted Jesus as their Lord and Savior and had not been in the church for five years, they didn't even know what we meant by reach people for Christ and give to the kingdom—which was huge because we had a lot of staff and customers who had never accepted Jesus as their Lord and Savior. So we had to change it up so everyone could feel a part while not diluting the truth of the gospel. Understand, our purpose never changes. But now, we say we do this by "helping them find their way home. By being a joyful, hope-filled, loving guide" so that everyone is a part of the process and also feels like they are.

These were some of the responsibilities God laid on my heart. I had to continue to mature in four ways: spiritually, relationally, physically, and financially.

This was part of the change God was continuing to make in me by transforming my mind, my heart, and my way of living, speaking, and thinking. And just like at home where I had to live out the change before my family, I had to allow the people I worked with to see the transformation rather than simply announce one day, "Look at me! I've changed!" I had to live differently, in a way that reflected the change in my heart. The process would take years, and it is ongoing.

To begin the transformation of the company, we laid out a plan we called Better Before Bigger, which emphasizes discipline, focus, and unity. An image that I shared many times over the course of three years was of the fishermen in Bible times who regularly mended their nets, repairing holes so they wouldn't lose fish. We were mending holes in our nets, in some cases completely throwing out an old net and getting a new one.

One of the most visible changes we made with the company was going from more than eighty house plans on our website to thirteen plans. Fewer plans allowed us to streamline the building process so we could finish quality homes more effectively and efficiently so we could also more effectively and efficiently achieve our mission.

We also changed the way many of our salaried employees were paid, moving to a system that based their income on the company's profitability. I knew the Lord was telling us to do this, but I was afraid that change could cause 30 to 40 percent of our staff to leave, because there would be no guaranteed salary. Instead, less than 2 percent left.

This was encouraging to me because I realized we had done a good job of hiring people who were a strong culture fit and who believed in our mission. We had also worked hard to communicate with them in a way that helped them see themselves as a valued part of the company.

As the company changed, I had to continue to grow as a man of God, husband, father, and leader. For example, for a long time in my life, I felt God was directing everything I did. He told me through prayer or His Word, "Go do this, and go do that." I felt God was telling me specifically what to do in particular situations.

Then as the company grew and my responsibilities grew with it, I didn't have enough time in the day to come pray and ask what to do in every situation that came up. *Do You want me to do this? Do You want me to do that?*

That's when I felt God saying to me, "You know My heart. You know My character. You know My Word. Now go and make the wisest decision based on those things. You will not get it perfect, but go and I will guide you as you follow Me."

Instead of directing every decision, He was delegating some of them.

Now I find the healthiest place for me to live is somewhere in the middle of Him directing me and Him delegating. When I face a major decision that impacts a lot of people and their families or requires a major investment of time or money, then I want to make sure I have a really clear word from God, His Word, and wise counsel.

For example, we owned a company, and I felt God telling us to give that company to the people who were running it. That's not something you do without being clear about God's specific instructions. We knew it lined up with the Word, but we also needed wise counsel. Then He told us to sell another company for what we had invested in it and to owner-finance the sale at a low interest rate.

Other times He has said, "Go make the best decision you can, but understand it's still Mine. You do the thing you think I would want—you are stewarding it for Me."

Now I'm trying to change my way of thinking, based on the model God is giving me, to be more empowering and less controlling. He is blessing me and empowering me to do His work. If the leaders of our companies and I can empower the people who work with us to make good decisions without asking us what they should do, except for big decisions, that's a game changer. It takes so much pressure off the leaders, who can spend more time adding value to our teams and on the vision, and it allows others to grow.

We created systems and processes that gave employees more ownership of their work and of the outcome. We had no idea where God was headed with all this, but three years into it, God told me He wanted

Tracy and me to sell the company to the employees. That's when we created an employee stock ownership plan for the employees to buy the company over ten years.

I realize now that the Better Before Bigger process, which was difficult for our employees, actually prepared them to become owners (or I should say stewards since God is still the real owner).

PREPARED FOR THE COVID SHUTDOWN

When COVID plunged into our world in 2020, God took me to Psalm 91. I believe this was a promise from Him to me personally but also to our entire family of companies. The Message version states in verses 9–10 and 14, "Because GOD's your refuge, the High God your very own home, evil can't get close to you, harm can't get through the door… 'If you'll hold on to me for dear life,' says GOD, 'I'll get you out of any trouble. I'll give you the best of care if you'll only get to know and trust me.'"

All the changes we had made through Better Before Bigger allowed us to become more technologically savvy and more virtually interactive with our website. At the time, the reason for these changes was to become more efficient. None of us had a clue how important those efficiencies would be to us in our time of social distancing. But God had a clue, and He prepared us long before we even knew why. He was protecting us before we knew we even needed protection. He was faithful to His promises even when we were not aware.

At the beginning of COVID, many homebuilders began scaling back and slowing down to see what would happen with market trends. We continued to pray over our own strategy, and I kept hearing God say that His vision for us in 2020 wasn't changing—that we were to keep doing what we were doing. So we continued to plow ahead, and business boomed, exceeding our budget goals in all companies.

The market grew so much that we had contracts to build way more houses than our strategic plan called for. That's a good thing, right? Building more houses this year moves us closer to our long-term goal. Everything we do at our companies begins with our vision. If we sell more homes, we reach more people, we increase our profit, and we give more to God's kingdom. But it's not that simple or clear. If we overextend ourselves on homes to the point where we can't perform at the highest level, we disappoint our customers and miss the opportunity to fulfill the relational part of our vision.

In the homebuilding industry, and just about any other business, there are times when what appears to be a super harvest of opportunity in front of you ends up biting you because you can get ahead of God's plan. That's when you have to slow down and ask, *Okay, God, what are we supposed to be doing now?*

Maybe this time of unexpected growth is part of God's plan for the business. In our case, we felt God telling us to stay focused on our three-year strategic plan. We discerned our three-year goals, which we discerned through prayer and wise counsel, and kept them in front of us until God told us to make a change.

We decided to slow down the sales, and we went for a period without making any sales at all. That alleviated some pressure for our teams, subcontractors, and vendors and allowed us to do a better job and still hit our financial target.

Another miracle of protection happened within our land development company. With the housing market flux, many land development companies experienced interruption with their scheduled lot purchases, affecting their overall profits. Yet all the homebuilders in contract with our development company had already completed their lot takedowns prior to the market disruption. Our development company wasn't affected by the disruption at all. We never could have planned this on our own. I saw it as God's provision and protection.

One of the most important miracles to me related to our giving goal. Every year, we set a giving goal for kingdom-minded projects. Earlier in the year, I started to feel in my spirit that God was going to blow our goal out of the water. I felt that we were going to be blessed enough to be able to give 150 percent of our goal for the year. We didn't know how that would be possible, but we just kept believing in faith that God was going to make it happen somehow. Sure enough, through the pandemic, the government instituted a new bill for this year that removed the charitable giving cap on businesses. Money that would have been tied up in taxes could instead be donated.

When challenges require adjustments today, I'm thinking about how I can mend that net in a way that will fix the problem today and also help us stay on target with our long-term plan while always aligning with our purpose. That way we continue to get better even in the midst of trials.

I look back and see that God had been with me through the most difficult times of my life, and I know I can trust Him and make Him my cornerstone. No matter what I encounter in life, He is unshakable. His perspective is always bigger than the trials and opportunities I am facing today. I try to see His impact in real time, through prayer and reading Scripture, but I

also humble myself and know I will not always get it
right but that when I fail, I can look back and see that
God was with me all the time. He will never leave me.

NO GREATER
LOVE

*I*n 2021, Tracy and I walked through a season where God asked us to take a step of faith to lay down our lives sacrificially to save one of His children. But it wasn't my life that was at risk. It was, potentially, Tracy's.

It began at an executive team meeting, when Terry Trayvick asked all of us to pray for their son, Myles, who needed a kidney transplant. Myles was twenty-three years old, and Terry had given him one of his kidneys eighteen years earlier. Myles's kidneys were now failing to the point that he was experiencing seizures because of the toxins accumulating. Terry said he needed a transplant. However, because there are so many more people in need of kidneys than there are donors, the wait can be as long as five years.

At those times, we naturally think of our own children and the possibility that we might lose them, and we believe that God will carry us through those valleys. God was giving strength to Terry and Sandy as they supported Myles. They would continue to believe, no matter what happened. We also all knew that God responds to prayers, so we prayed together and later in our one-on-one times with God that He would heal

Myles or that He would touch the heart of a donor who would be a match.

Two days later, Tracy and I were talking about Myles, and she said, "I think God wants me to give Myles one of my kidneys."

Really? I immediately thought, but I swallowed the words before they came out.

Tracy could read my fearful thoughts in my expression. "I think so," she said.

Tracy is my wife and my best friend, and I couldn't imagine losing her. Donating a kidney, obviously, requires major surgery. She would be risking her life for Myles. And what if she had problems with her remaining kidney down the road? But I also know Tracy's relationship with the Lord.

"I know you hear from God," I said, "and if that's what God is telling you, I support you all the way."

Without telling Tracy, I went to my prayer closet and told God, *You're going to have to speak this to me, and You're going to have to give me a word on this.*

He gave me Psalm 24:1:

The earth is the LORD's, and everything in it,
the world, and all who live in it.

Through that verse, He was telling me that we belong to God—every part of us belongs to God. He says to "love the Lord your God with all your heart and with all your soul and with all your mind and with all your strength" (Mark 12:30), and that means with our body, our organs—everything down the marrow of our bones.

My understanding of Psalm 24:1 was incomplete, and that's the beauty of Scripture. We can continue to grow and see things that we did not before. Everything is the Lord's, the psalm says, including the kidneys inside Tracy's body. God said to me, "I simply asked Tracy if she would take what's already Mine and allow Me to give it to Myles."

So Tracy wasn't donating a kidney, God was.

Tracy said yes.

When Tracy was a child, her cousin underwent a kidney transplant. Tracy told her if she ever needed another one, she would give her one of hers. Tracy remembered that moment and realized God had been preparing her to be a kidney donor all those years ago—she thought it would be for her cousin, but now she realized it was for Myles. It's crazy to think that Tracy and Myles didn't even know each other. In fact, Myles had not even been born yet, but God was planting this seed in Tracy's heart.

Despite God's hand on Tracy, the process of donating a kidney would be difficult. Tracy hates going to the doctor. She had never undergone surgery, and her only time in the hospital as a patient was when our children were born.

God reassured her through her prayers that He was in control. She told her parents, and like Tracy, they trusted God to protect her. And when she told Ashtyn, our daughter, she replied, "If you're not a match, should I try?"

Tracy began to tear up, and she told her, "I think you need to let me get through this." She was not without concern for the possibilities, even with God in control.

Tracy was a match, and she was not alone in her willingness to share. She learned that two other members of our staff had already been tested to see if they might be matches, but they were not.

I continued to trust God, but at the same time I asked Him for another way—even healing Myles's kidney. I did not want to lose Tracy, and I believe we can pray that way without guilt. Even Jesus prayed for another way in the garden of Gethsemane on the night before He was crucified.

"I'm not asking you and Tracy to do anything that I haven't done," He said. "When I shed My blood, I was giving up My flesh."

So we traveled to New Jersey, where the Trayvicks live, and the morning of the surgery Chad texted to all of us Deuteronomy 31:8:

> The LORD himself goes before you and will be with you; he will never leave you nor forsake you. Do not be afraid; do not be discouraged.

Terry texted back, "Sandy wanted me to let you know that God is speaking to Joshua in Deuteronomy 31:8. What you probably didn't know is Joshua is Myles's middle name. Hallelujah!"

God is in the details, as Chad would say later. He is meticulous in His love for us, and He gave us exactly the right word at the right time. I waited with Terry and Sandy when they took Tracy back and then Myles, and the surgeon came out later and said all had gone well.

Tracy and Myles were in rooms beside each other, so we had something like a family time together.

Of course, we *are* family, especially now. After this experience, we feel family in a different way. I don't know how to explain that difference. God just blows me away when I think of the journey that He's taken us on so far and the people that He has put in our life.

When God introduced me to Terry all those years ago, I knew He wanted us to work together. Now we see that it was also about Myles.

When God brought Tracy into my life thirty years ago, I didn't know how to love the way God wanted to love. He guided me day by day, year by year, even today, as you have read in these pages.

Then God used Tracy to show me what He meant. Through my wife, God showed me how to love as Jesus commanded.

> *This is my command: Love one another the way I loved you. This is the very best way to love. Put your life on the line for your friends.*
>
> —JOHN 15:12–13 (MSG)

For God so loved the world, that he gave his only begotten Son, that whosoever believeth in him should not perish, but have everlasting life.

—JOHN 3:16 (KJV)

MY PRAYER
AT FIFTY

*I*turned fifty years old when I was writing this book, and on that morning, Tracy reminded me of something I had told her twenty-seven years earlier. One of my goals in life was to be able to retire at fifty—to have that choice. I had totally forgotten I'd said that.

Two weeks earlier in a conversation with Chad, we were discussing all the opportunities and difficulties created by COVID and so many other stressors of the day, and he said, "You realize, John, you don't have to work anymore. You can do whatever you want."

He wasn't saying I had more money than I'd ever want or need. The companies were running pretty smoothly, and I didn't have to be in the day to day. We had worked hard to develop our leaders and culture. Our leaders could keep that going.

Whatever you want.

What does that even mean?

When I was twelve or thirteen years old, God told the pastor at our church in Waco that it was time for him to retire. Our pastor agreed to step down after he had selected and trained a replacement. The church board agreed, and they set the plan in motion.

Then about a year and a half into the process, our pastor said he was not pleased with the man he had selected as a replacement. He fired the man and announced that he was going to remain pastor of the church after all. In time the church dissolved.

I remembered that pastor when God told me to step down as CEO, after we had put John Houston Homes into an employee stock ownership plan for employees to own and control.

Our board and I decided I should stay on in a consulting role, and I asked them to research and determine an appropriate, market-based payment for that position. They did and said the right number would be about 18 percent of my salary as CEO. And because the economy was tight, they wondered if I would be willing to defer the payment.

Well, this was the first time I struggled with the idea of letting go of the company and my position as CEO. I asked myself, *So is my value to the company 82 percent less today than it was yesterday?*

I went to God and asked, *Why do I feel this way?* and the Lord asked in response, "Why are you asking that question? Is your value in money? Is your value in how much you make? Is your value in your title?"

He reminded me of the pastor—a story I probably shouldn't even have been aware of as a kid. Then He told me, "Son, you're not dealing with the emotions of a pay cut or a title change, because I have been taking care of you forever, every hour of every day, and I continue to remind you that you are a son of the living God and I love you. You're dealing with an abandonment issue that goes all the way back to your childhood." God was referring to the fact that my older brother and I lived alone as teenagers after our parents divorced. It took years for me to understand—and God is still helping me understand—that although we may feel abandoned by people in our lives, even by companies, He will never leave me nor forsake me.

"I had you start this company, this 'family,' and through you, I built it," He continued, "Then I asked you to die to yourself, take up your cross, and follow Me for the employees and their families for generations to come. You held on to this CEO position that kept you a part of the family. Now you don't have that position anymore, and you feel like they're abandoning you."

Of course, that was not the case. In fact, I believe God is using this transition to prepare me for a new thing.

"Trust Me," He said. "Stop relying on yourself, and trust Me."

I trusted enough to let go of the company and to let go of my position. Will I ever trust God completely? In this life? I wish I could say yes with confidence.

But here's what God has shown me: when I let go of the old ways, He allows me to experience the new that He has prepared. This is a pruning process so the employees and this company and I can bear more fruit. He was teaching me to remain in Him and He would remain in me. No branch can bear fruit without remaining in the vine. I think this has been much of the lesson He has been teaching me—to remain in Him, to let Him be my source, my sustenance, then I can bear much fruit. I know I have much more to learn on this, but I think that is a powerful lesson He is still teaching me.

God has spent nearly thirty years teaching me to trust and preparing me for what is next in my journey with Him, not for my glory but for His, because He wants me to know Him, His love, His mercy, His grace, His faithfulness, and more, so then I can go bear more abundant and healthier fruit by passing this on to others.

As I considered what Tracy and Chad had said, I thought about the desires of the heart of my twenty-three-year-old self. At that age, I trusted the resources I could gather to allow me to retire at fifty.

Now that I'm here, I realize the message God has for me is, "Son, I love you, I love you, I love you, and I am pleased with you, not because of what you do for Me, but because that is who I am! Now, trust Me more, remaining in Me and I in you."

My desire at twenty-three was mostly about me and the stuff I wanted. I wasn't mature enough spiritually to understand what God was putting on my heart. God has been teaching me—softening my heart, so I can know, hear, and understand Him more clearly. His purpose has been to help me to know His love and faithfulness more and to share this through the company and influence He has given me—to bring people to Himself for His glory. He has been teaching me what being blessed to be a blessing looks like.

We started out with one small homebuilding company with a few employees and subcontractors. Today, God has grown us into a family of companies centered on the homebuying experience, with hundreds of employees, subcontractors, and vendors.

Every day, throughout the companies, we have hundreds of opportunities to share the love of Christ by sharing the hope that is within us with gentleness and respect.

In another thirty or forty years, however long I live, if I can continue to grow in Christ, continue to have God search my heart, continue to ask God to show me His love and grow my trust in Him, how much different can my life look then versus today? How much grace can He give me, and how much more grace can I give?

The love and power of God changing one issue at a time in my heart has built on itself, like the power of compound interest. Growth was slow at first, but over time, the pace increased, or maybe it just seems like it has, because I no longer resist it but try to embrace it. When He revealed another issue to work on, it was as if He was allowing me to invest in a new change that sometimes came a little quicker because of the changes that preceded it.

Now, I can honestly say my prayer is this:

Lord Jesus, thank You for blessing me with Your love and relationship with You, the Lord God

Almighty. Thank You for dying on the cross so I can be forgiven and spend eternity with You. Lord, search my heart and reveal the evil desires of my heart to me and help me to turn from them before they manifest themselves into sin. Please don't give me more than I can handle, that I would turn from You, and please don't give me less, that I might not fulfill the hopes and the plans in the future that You have for me. Because ultimately all I want to do is please You, that Your love, glory, and honor may be known to others. Amen.

ACKNOWLEDGMENTS

I believe God wanted me to tell the story of how He led me to build businesses to reach people for Christ and give to the Kingdom. He used many experiences to help me come to trust and love Him even more through the process. But I'm a businessman more than a writer. So the book you are reading was made possible by an amazing group of people who offered me their expertise and support.

Dick Parker is a gifted communicator and helped me take all of my thoughts and stories and put them together in a way that I never could have done on my own. I appreciate Dick for being such a trusted partner and friend.

Jonathan Merkh and Jen Gingerich from Forefront have done a great job, once again, as my publishers. They wisely led me through each step and provided great editorial advice.

Aunie Brooks and Holly Moore guided the process from the time we sat around my dining room table and dreamed of the idea for this book until the completion. I'm grateful for the way they believed in me, and the message Jesus wanted to tell. They truly helped bring it to life.

The Executive Team at the John Houston Family of Companies is the best group of leaders I have ever had the privilege of serving with in my career. My wife, Tracy, Terry, Chad, Bobby, and Charity are intelligent, wise, and generous in the way they use their gifts to pursue the vision the Lord has given us.

I want to thank my family for their constant love and support. Being Austin and Ashtyn's father and friend is such an incredible honor. They are beginning to launch out into the plans and purpose God has for their lives, and I love seeing them do what God created them to do.

Tracy is my wife and my best friend. We are entering into a new season in our lives, and I can't wait to see all

God has in store for us together. Wherever He leads us is good as long as you are by my side. You are an amazing woman of God, wife, mother, and leader, and I am humbled to follow Jesus with you. Thank you for loving me, respecting me, and supporting me in such an amazing way.